Charles Dickens

A LIPPER™/VIKING BOOK

GENERAL EDITOR: JAMES ATLAS

JANE SMILEY

Charles Dickens

A Penguin Life

A LIPPER™/VIKING BOOK

VIKING
Published by the Penguin Group
Penguin Putnam Inc., 375 Hudson Street,
New York, New York 10014, U.S.A.
Penguin Books Ltd, 80 Strand, London WC2R 0RL, England
Penguin Books Australia Ltd, 250 Camberwell Road, Camberwell,
Victoria 3124, Australia
Penguin Books Canada Ltd, 10 Alcorn Avenue,
Toronto, Ontario, Canada M4V 3B2
Penguin Books India (P) Ltd, 11 Community Centre, Panchsheel Park,
New Delhi–110 017, India
Penguin Books (N.Z.) Ltd, Cnr Rosedale and Airborne Roads, Albany,
Auckland, New Zealand
Penguin Books (South Africa) (Pty) Ltd, 24 Sturdee Avenue,
Rosebank, Johannesburg 2196, South Africa

Penguin Books Ltd, Registered Offices:
Harmondsworth, Middlesex, England

First published in 2002 by Viking Penguin,
a member of Penguin Putnam Inc.

1   3   5   7   9   10   8   6   4   2

LIBRARY OF CONGRESS CATALOGING-IN-PUBLICATION DATA
Smiley, Jane.
Charles Dickens / Jane Smiley.
p.   cm.—(Penguin lives series)
"A Penguin life."
"A Lipper/Viking book."
ISBN 0-670-03077-5
1. Dickens, Charles, 1812–1870.   2. Novelists, English—
19th century—Biography.   I. Title.   II. Series.
PR4581.S616 2002
823'.8—dc21
[B]   2001045607

This book is printed on acid-free paper. ∞

Printed in the United States of America
Set in Adobe Garamond   •   Designed by Francesca Belanger

Preface

THE LITERARY SENSIBILITY of Charles Dickens is possibly the most amply documented literary sensibility in history. Not only did he write fifteen novels, ten of which were eight hundred or more pages long, he also wrote numerous stories, articles, travel pieces, essays, letters, editorial notes, and plays. For his entire literary life, he was observed by relatives, friends, servants, acquaintances, fellow authors, and strangers, who wrote about him in reviews, articles, diaries, letters, biographies, memoirs, and autobiographies. He was relentlessly observed by himself, sometimes sympathetically, sometimes unsympathetically. He was, in short, an object of fascination, a true celebrity (maybe the first true celebrity in the modern sense), a social phenomenon, a figure unique among his contemporaries and yet representative of them, as they themselves understood. Among English writers, Dickens's only peer, in terms of general fame, worldwide literary stature, and essential Englishness, is William Shakespeare, and the two authors are alike in several ways. Both peopled the imaginative landscape in a manner almost superhuman, pouring forth characters of such number, variety, and vividness that it seems impossible that they could be the products of a single mind. Both depicted English life when English life was at its most interesting and vital, and both seemed to sparkle at the center of that life, in London, though both were also adept at evoking English pastoral scenes. They share another quality, too, and that is that both remain essentially mysterious, Shakespeare in part because so little is known of him outside of his plays, and Dickens in part because everything that is known of him makes him all the more difficult to comprehend.

Biographies of Dickens, long and short, abound. A lifelong friend of his, John Forster, published the first authoritative one shortly after Dickens died. The most recent, by Peter Ackroyd, published in 1990, is more than a thousand pages long. It is, therefore, not the intention of this volume to lay out chronologically everything that we have come to know of Charles Dickens's life as a result of some 130 years of industrious digging on the part of aficionados and scholars from all parts of the world (though admittedly mostly from England). The Charles Dickens we know is decidedly different from the man his contemporaries knew. For one thing, Dickens did not reveal the details of his painful childhood even to his children, and he did not come to terms with it himself until he chose to revisit his early experiences while writing *David Copperfield.* He kept other secrets as well. Rather than telling his story chronologically, I will attempt to evoke Dickens as he might have seemed to his contemporary audience, to friends and relatives, to intimate acquaintances, to himself, filling in the background only as he became willing to address it in his work. My purpose here is to avoid the dreary illusion of superiority that comes when critics and biographers purport to know a subject better than (or more truthfully than or more insightfully than) the subject knew himself. Writers and artists are often portrayed as carriers of their own works, rather like carriers of disease, who communicate them to the world at large unconsciously, giving themselves away without design or intention. My own experience as a writer and a reader is quite different. Writing is an act of artistic and moral agency, where choices are made that the author understands, full of implications and revelations that the author also understands. One thing that we know about Dickens from his editorial work is that he had an exceptionally sophisticated understanding of how writing works—of what is appealing and why, of the balance between the artistic and the commercial, of how to create effects, and of the competing claims of morality, aesthetics, and truth in the composition and social function of serious fiction, as well as the other forms of literature that Dickens turned his attention to. We also know that Dickens was quite well aware of the impression he made upon those around him and was adept at manipulating it. Acting was his great avocation from first to last, and he worked as hard at the presentation of his works, and of himself, as he did at his writing and editing.

In addition, I will offer interpretations of almost all of Dickens's major works. One of the most interesting things about Charles Dickens is the way in which his style and his interest in social themes remained remarkably consistent throughout his career, while his vision shifted and evolved. His Christmas books, for example, offer a different philosophical solution to the dilemmas presented by capitalism than do his great novels of the 1850s, *Bleak House* and *Little Dorrit*. Dickens was intently and systematically engaged with the social and economic questions of his time. He passionately sought solutions for such practical issues as public sanitation and relief of want and ignorance; he also pondered death, evil, cruelty, innocence, comfort, pleasure, happiness, and redemption. And he was an endlessly witty man, for whom words were a permanent delight. His novels shaped his life as much as his life shaped his novels, and just as his novels were in part commentary on his life, so his actions, in part, grew out of the way that writing novels gave his feelings and thoughts specific being. To a novelist, his work is not his product but his experience. Over time, his readers are further and further removed from the details of his life, but while they are reading his books, they are in his presence, experiencing his process of thought and imagination as it precipitates inchoate idea to particular word. To me, this is the miracle of literature, that minds can communicate, can meditate upon the same images, across decades, centuries, and miles. Charles Dickens was so thoroughly a novelist that we can hardly know him at all without following him into every novel.

Let us, then, not approach the man himself with a hostile desire to catch him out in self-contradictions and failures of self-knowledge, but rather with a friendly desire to get to know him and to achieve what Victorians might have termed "a growing intimacy."

Charles Dickens

CHAPTER ONE

CHARLES DICKENS was a public man and a famous man, and he assumed both of these slightly different roles in his early twenties. His first sketch, "A Dinner at Poplar Walk," was published in the *Monthly Magazine* in December 1833. Dickens, born on February 7, 1812, was only twenty-one, but because of his work as a parliamentary reporter (he had taught himself shorthand and was able to take down speeches word for word), he was already familiar with seeing his name in print. Nevertheless, he related later that "I walked down to Westminster Hall, and turned into it for half an hour, because my eyes were so dimmed with joy and pride, that they could not bear the street, and were not fit to be seen there." Further sketches published in monthly and weekly magazines over the following months attracted considerable notice, and when *Sketches by Boz* appeared in volume form in February and December 1836, they were well reviewed. What everyone, including Dickens himself, considered especially remarkable was their breadth of scope, and in particular the variety of lower-class characters and scenes depicted, perhaps a first in English literature. One reviewer called them "a perfect picture of the morals, manners, and habits of a great portion of English Society."

At only twenty-four, Dickens found himself in an advantageous authorial position—he was invited to contribute the text for a series of sporting engravings to be published by the firm of Chapman and Hall. They offered Dickens £14 per month (it is impossible to know exactly what this would be equivalent to in modern dollars, but it is useful to multiply any Dickensian sum by 35, which would make his fee about $500). The artist, Robert Seymour, was successful and famous, and it was he who was supposed to take the lead in conceiving and guiding the collaboration. The arrangement lasted two months, until Seymour committed suicide. In even this short a time, though, Dickens was able to assert his own resolve that he should direct the project, and by the time another artist, Hablot Browne, was hired, Dickens had gotten himself a raise, increased the proportion of the writing to the illustrations, and turned the whole endeavor into *The Pickwick Papers,* which was destined to become a publishing phenomenon.

The Pickwick Papers was published between March 1836 and November 1837. From that time to the end of his life, Charles Dickens was a figure of whom everyone had something to say, so it is appropriate to take a look at him upon his first real entrance into the condition of celebrity. First and foremost, friends and acquaintances noted his lively presence, his charm, his good looks, and his colorful style of dress. Though rather short, and even slight, Dickens was extremely straight in his bearing, and his friend and future biographer John Forster recalled "the quickness, keenness, and practical power, the eager, restless, energetic outlook. . . . Light and motion flashed from every part of it." Forster asserted that humor, "habitual, unbounded, and resistless," was his most essential characteristic, but everyone he knew expressed astonishment at Dickens's level of activity, whether the object of that activity was work, games, exercise, amateur acting and play production, charitable projects, or anything else. He was good company and he loved all sociable amusements. He later commented that at this time of his life he was going out to the theater sometimes every night of the week—not only to see the more respectable offerings at Covent Garden and Drury Lane, but to any and all sorts of shows, spectacles, pageants, and performances. Himself adept at declaiming, singing, and performing, he was invited everywhere and participated fully in all forms of the social life of the time—parties and "at homes," nights on the town with groups of male friends, dinners, jaunts, impromptu adventures. Already, though, observers were finding something uncanny about his manner. As astute as he was charming, he often gave people the sense that they were being "scanned" from top to bottom. Extant portraits and photographs certainly fail to reveal the Dickens that his contemporaries knew, especially in the early years, since for various technical reasons subjects were never pictured or photographed smiling. It is especially important, therefore, to be mindful that what the twenty-first century is able to *see* of Dickens is the merest brittle shell of how he appeared to those around him.

The Pickwick Papers sold fewer than 500 copies of the first monthly number. The fourth number sold 4,000, the eleventh 14,000, and the last numbers around 40,000. Once published in volume form, it sold well for the rest of Dickens's life and after. By 1878, it had sold 1.6 million copies in various editions.

The success of his literary efforts enabled Dickens to progress in his private life, and on the second of April 1836, he married Catherine Hogarth, the daughter of George Hogarth, the editor of the newly established *Evening Chronicle,* a journal to which Dickens contributed twenty pieces. The Hogarths were Scottish, and before becoming a journalist George had been a lawyer in Edinburgh and the legal adviser and intimate friend of Walter Scott, an author Dickens very much admired. Catherine was the eldest of nine children, and the Hogarths were a lively, clever family. George himself was an accomplished musician and served as music critic of another newspaper that Dickens had written for, the *Morning Chronicle.*

The twenty-four-year-old Dickens embraced the Hogarth family and, in turn, was embraced by them. He was impressed with their cultural connections, their liveliness, and their talents, especially the musical ones, which Dickens had a particular affinity for, being himself a performer and ready singer of popular songs, and he treated not only George but also Mrs. Hogarth with great affection. It may have seemed to him that he had found the one family that perfectly reflected his own aspirations to a hardworking prominence that was both artistic and bourgeois. An earlier suit had failed. His beloved, a young woman named Maria Beadnell, daughter of a banker, whom he had courted obsessively for four years, had finally rejected him (or her connections had broken off the relationship—the circumstances remain unclear) in May 1833.

Catherine Hogarth was a placid and gentle young woman of twenty quite unlike Maria Beadnell. Dickens's letters to her show that he felt affectionate toward Catherine, though not especially passionate, and that he took directing and molding her as seriously as he took pleasing and courting her—he was moving eagerly into the accepted Victorian role of pater-familias. He also grew quite fond of, and intimate with, Catherine's younger sister Mary, who moved in with the young couple. His marriage and his relationship with the Hogarths, then, nicely expressed who he thought himself to be at the time, as well as his ideal of family life—a sort of cozy, busy, fecund, sociable, and comfortable household where people with imagination, energy, and considerable social mobility could gather and find both enjoyment and stimulation. The family formed by Charles, Catherine, and Mary seems to have suited all of them, and for Dickens it was as close as he ever came to domestic happiness. The gentle and affectionate, but somewhat languid Catherine satisfied the role of wife and mother, while the quicker Mary offered a more virginal and intellectual form of female companionship.

By the age of twenty-four, Dickens had already been working for nine years. He had applied himself to every task with vigor, and through a mixture of indefatigable endeavor, talent, imagination, charm, and focus, he had succeeded at nearly everything he tried. Only his great passion for acting had been stymied: on the day of his audition as a professional actor, he had fallen ill with a cold. Publication, of course, and the huge success of *Pickwick* fixed his professional course, but he could never be said to have "failed" at acting—he came back to it over and over, in amateur theatricals and other per-formances, and always received excellent reviews. In addition, in this same period, he became friends with William Charles Macready, one of the greatest actors of the Victorian period, a man who did much to rehabilitate the plays of William

Shakespeare from the corrupted versions common in the eighteenth century.

Foremost among Dickens's friends was John Forster, another literary bon vivant and another ambitious and self-made man. Dickens and Forster were close associates in every way for the rest of Dickens's life, in personal, artistic, and public affairs. Forster handled many of Dickens's business matters, was his artistic and editorial adviser on many projects, and at last wrote the first and in some ways the most exhaustive (though discreet) Dickens biography. There were plenty of other friends, mostly artists, authors, and other men of the artistic/public sort.

Dickens's own family was like an unsuccessful version of the Hogarth family. John Dickens was a skilled journalist, also of a convivial temperament, and considered to be a man of some charm. Of Elizabeth Dickens, too, it was said that she was vivacious and winning. But the elder Dickenses had led a life of such improvidence, marked by so many changes in circumstances, that Charles Dickens's attitude toward them, both together and individually, was at the very least extremely complex and in some ways a contrast to his general charitableness. In the early years of his marriage and professional success, he was tormented by the fecklessness as well as the importunities of his parents and his brothers. With success and marriage, he had separated himself from the life he had led with them (a life that he hardly ever spoke of), but he could not as easily separate himself from his relations themselves. He attempted to find them work, to find them places to live (sometimes at quite a distance), to keep them at arm's length, but he repeatedly found himself bailing them out of financial difficulties. This was especially true of his father, and Dickens often spoke of his parents with exasperation in letters to friends. Even so, for fifteen months, it seemed as though Charles and Catherine Dickens were especially favored in every way—Dickens was busy, rich, and popular. He knew at once and without being told how interconnected fame, money, influence, and artistic independence were, and he asserted himself almost immediately to sustain all four of them through hard work, aggressive business dealings, and self-promotion. And, of course, the exercise of genius.

Catherine Dickens gave birth to Charles junior on January 2, 1837, and in April the couple moved out of their rooms into a house. Then, on May 7, after an illness of only a few days, seventeen-year-old Mary Hogarth died suddenly. She died in Dickens's arms, and he was so undone by the loss that he had to put off completing the installment of *The Pickwick Papers* that he was working on. He wore one of her rings on his finger for the rest of his life and kept a lock of her hair and her clothes. When, five years later, one of her brothers died and was buried with her, Dickens wrote that "the thought of being excluded from her dust" was like "losing her a second time." Over the course of the next thirty years, he thought of her constantly and did not think that the influence of her spirit over him could be exaggerated. She is often said to have inspired several of Dickens's female characters of a certain type, of which Agnes, in *David Copperfield,* is an example— virtuous, compliant, and virginal, voiceless in a sense, and almost always too good for this world. Catherine could never take her place or fill, by herself, the two roles that Dickens needed filled by the women in his life.

. . .

The Pickwick Papers is not a book that holds much appeal for the modern reader. Episodic sporting adventures, however, were quite popular at the time, and a large part of their appeal was in the accompanying illustrations. The "novel" has the looseness and digressiveness of many eighteenth-century works like *Tom Jones* and *Tristram Shandy,* both of which Dickens admired. Dickens had not at that point developed his particular social vision, especially the darker, angrier parts of it, and his style, though already distinct, does not have the incandescent and concentrated ironic power that he achieved in later works. What he does have, full grown, and what readers noticed almost at once, is that facility in drawing characters that are not only entertaining but unique. An early example is Alfred Jingle, who joins Pickwick's party of friends and at first seems benign enough. His characteristic mode of expression is a sort of word-association utterance of disjointed cant phrases: "Splendid—capital. Kent, sir—everybody knows Kent—apples, cherries, hops, and women. Glass of wine, sir?" And a few moments later: "'Beg your pardon, sir,' said the stranger, 'bottle stands—pass it round—way of the sun—through the button-hole—no heeltaps.'" The Pickwickians are deceived by Jingle's bonhomie and apparent savoir faire, until he attempts to elope with the sister of their host. Only when he is being bought off by the man's lawyer does he speak in coherent sentences. When the lawyer suggests that £50 is a "good round sum—a man like you could treble it in no time—great deal to be done with fifty pounds, my dear sir," Jingle has no trouble responding "coolly," "More to be done with a hundred and fifty." Jingle's mode of expression is funny in itself, partly because it is mechanical and repetitive in rhythm and partly because the associated phrases are unexpected, and the shift to a more normal speech pattern reveals and underscores Jingle's duplicity. This is the absolute heart of Charles Dickens's idiosyncratic genius: what Jingle communicates to the reader, and what Dickens communicates through him, accumulates meanings and layers with every piece of dialogue and is simultaneously interesting and economical. And Jingle's style stands in contrast with the narrator's and the Pickwickians' more discursive manner, adding yet another layer.

Throughout his life, Dickens had a superb talent for mimicry, for speaking in voices, that almost amounted to allowing the voices all around him to speak through him. It was a talent he cultivated, but also himself marveled at, telling Forster that his characters came to him and spoke through him. David Lodge, one of the foremost comic novelists of our own day, and an experienced theorist, has written in *After Bakhtin* that the only way successfully to come to terms with the variety and scope of the novel is through analyzing it as a chorus of individual voices speaking in varying styles and tones, rather than as a single rhetorical expression. This is certainly true of Dickens as much as or more than any other novelist. But it is important to remember, too, that all of these voices are filtered through Dickens's consciousness, that every character is Dickens, whoever happened to be the original inspiration. Otherwise it is impossible to come to any comprehension of the variety, and variability, of the man himself.

Perhaps the most famous and best-loved character in *The Pickwick Papers* is Sam Weller. In the first few numbers of

The Pickwick Papers, Dickens ascribes qualities of wisdom and benevolence to Pickwick himself, and to his friends, but these qualities remain rather abstract until the introduction of Sam, who is eloquently easygoing, street smart, and kindly. He is a foil for Pickwick's own bland innocence, and he provides commentary on what could easily become a series of meaningless episodes. His voice substitutes for the voice of the narrator, which the young Dickens has not yet mastered as he soon will. Sam Weller's voice is free, whereas the narrator's voice is still inhibited by middle-class convention and eighteenth-century diction. The innate skill for writing compelling voices that Dickens shows so well with Jingle and several of the other characters he practices and develops in Sam Weller. As soon as he introduced, he is interesting: "Well, you *are* a nice young 'ooman for a musical party, you are. Look at these her boots—eleven pair o' boots; and one shoe as b'longs to number six, with the wooden leg. . . ." His dialogue has accent and rhythm; it expresses his character while showing what he is doing and what he has observed. He adds something unexpected to the narrative every time he opens his mouth. Very soon after Sam appears and disappears, the Pickwickians witness the Eatanswill election. In this scene we have the beginnings of Dickensian social satire. The narrative style is slightly more ironic than earlier, but neither the narrator nor Pickwick himself can assume such an ironic voice without materially changing how they have already been presented. It is no coincidence that Sam returns to the narrative soon after, the perfect solution to the problem of how to comment upon the events of the narrative without betraying the tone of what has gone before. That the introduction of Sam

Weller coincided with the rise in sales of the serial numbers indicates that through him Dickens had found his marriage of story and theme—great variety and breadth of incident plus overt, but comically expressed, social commentary. This form would remain constant to the end of Dickens's life, changing in mood and balance, but always constituting what we consider to be quintessentially "Dickensian."

No author's life is a strand of pearls, with books or plays or poems strung in a neat sequence upon a smooth string of personal events, but Dickens's life is even less sequential than most. Events and projects cascaded over one another, each requiring the author's intensive focus. He did not write the two volumes of *Sketches,* and then *Pickwick,* and then *Oliver Twist,* and so on. Rather, he was still gathering together the *Sketches* while he was writing *Pickwick,* and *Oliver Twist* began to run as a serial before *Pickwick* had finished. He was also writing essays and articles, and in some of them can be seen the germs of characters or ideas that are later developed more extensively in the novels. And during the extremely productive period of the late 1830s, Charles Dickens threw himself into two other activities that were to shape much of the rest of his life. One of these was editing.

In the autumn of 1836, publisher Richard Bentley approached Dickens with a plan for a new monthly magazine that Dickens would edit, and in January 1837, Dickens introduced the first number. This was the author's first experience wearing a hat he would continue to wear for many decades. He was no figurehead, but a very active and opinionated director of all aspects of the magazine. He read and considered eighty manuscripts each month, then prepared them for publication. He even did the proofreading. When his relationship with Bentley broke down after only a few years, it was because he found Bentley too interfering, not because he felt overburdened by work (though he often felt overburdened by work). Dickens was always looking for control and autonomy, and his career was marked by ferocious battles with publishers over contracts, money, and independence. His correspondence with authors shows that he had specific and very strong views about how pieces should be written and what effect they should have. His views were both aesthetic and political—to make a piece more lively and interesting was also to take a stand against the mechanical dreariness that Dickens felt was overwhelming English life. He was always in favor of imagination and "fancy," always opposed to dullness and the ponderousness that was a mask for social cruelty. His success in depicting the variety of lower-class English life was no accident—he was both interested in the lower orders and eager to show them to themselves and to the middle and upper classes.

The first ten parts of *Oliver Twist* were written at the same time Dickens was writing the last ten parts of *Pickwick*. Each section of *Oliver Twist* ran to about eight thousand words, and each section of *Pickwick* ran to about twice that or a bit more, so Dickens was writing ninety pages a month of these novels, while also working on other essays, articles, speeches, and plays. Evidence is that he would write the dark, ironic chapters of *Oliver Twist* first, then the light, comic chapters of *Pickwick*. The death of Mary Hogarth caused him to miss the June number of both novels and, some critics say, to soften the harshness of *Oliver Twist;* but in spite of his profound mourning, he never stinted his activities.

All through 1836 and 1837—that is, while writing, editing, getting married, moving house, and having children (Mary, called Mamie, was born on March 6, 1838)—Dickens was also writing plays and promoting or overseeing their production. He wrote four dramatic works during this period: *The Strange Gentleman,* a comic piece; *The Village Coquettes,* an operetta; *Is She His Wife?,* a farce; and *The Lamplighter,* another farce. And though all of them went into production, and three of them had performances, only *The Strange Gentleman* ran for more than a handful of performances, and Dickens (reluctantly, perhaps) gave up playwriting for the time being. While not lasting works of art, the plays are testament both to Dickens's creative energy and to his surpassing love of the theater, which would emerge in later life in several potent ways.

Along with *A Christmas Carol, Oliver Twist* is probably the best known of Dickens's narratives, certainly because, like many of Dickens's own works and like many other nineteenth-century novels, it was reworked for the stage, where the simple and vivid story of the workhouse child who falls among thieves and then is rescued and restored to his own wealthy grandfather made a dramatic and cohesive play. The arc of the narrative is fairy tale–like, but the details of Oliver's companions and surroundings came directly from Dickens's immediate world. The New Poor Law, under which members of families were parted from one another according to gender, with the feeding regulations that Oliver so memorably flouts when he asks Mr. Bumble the beadle for more, had been in effect for some three years and was widely opposed by more liberal and radical elements of English society, of which Dickens counted himself one. The area of London where Fagin and his gang of thieves lived was very close to where Dickens lived while he was doing much of the writing, and Dickens, with his lifelong love of walking, was intimately familiar with it (as with most of London and, indeed, all of the places where he lived). Dickens's outrage at the primitive conditions that the poor of London had to live in was genuine, both on their behalf and as what we might term an "ecological understanding" that there could be no real separation between the rich and the poor, the healthy and the diseased, the dirty and the clean, the educated and the ignorant. Images of the flow of all things abound in his fiction from beginning to end, and in some sense he was always striving in his work to include more and more, to make each novel bigger and broader and also more particular, and to make the links between all things less linear and more netlike, to reproduce on the page the simultaneity and comprehensiveness of the way his mind and world around him joined.

Like *The Pickwick Papers, Oliver Twist* was related in form to other works that were popular at the time, in this case narratives of the lives of real orphans; but, according to Ackroyd, it was the first English novel to take a child as its protagonist. In some sense, *Oliver Twist* turned the world upside down and offered a new view of things to Dickens's readers—life at the bottom of Victorian society, as seen through the eyes of a child. The form allowed the author to approach at a distance issues of his own childhood that he was not yet ready to address, among them feelings of victimization and abandonment.

As a narrator, the author was openly satirical. Early in the novel, for example, when Oliver is apprenticed to the undertaker Sowerberry, he incurs the ire of Mr. Bumble the beadle by defending the honor of his unknown mother. Mr. Bumble declares that Oliver's spirit must come from too rich a diet. The narrator comments, "The liberality of Mrs. Sowerberry to Oliver had consisted in a profuse bestowal upon him of all the dirty odds and ends which nobody else would eat, so there was a great deal of meekness and self-devotion in her voluntarily remaining under Mr. Bumble's heavy accusation. Of which, to do her justice, she was wholly innocent in thought, word, and deed." And *Oliver Twist* is especially rich in dialogue (perhaps evidence of Dickens's concurrent playwriting); the objects of the author's scorn repeatedly satirize themselves: "'Have the goodness to look at me,' said Mr. Bumble, fixing his eyes upon [his wife]. ('If she stands such an eye as that,' said Mr. Bumble to himself, 'she can stand anything. It is an eye I never knew to fail with paupers. If it fails with her, my power is gone.')" But, of course, *Oliver Twist* is as famous for melodrama as for satire, and Dickens's ironic tone frequently gives way to something more sentimental (as with Mr. Brownlow and Rose Maylie) and to something more sinister (as with Bill Sikes and Monks). In fact, Oliver's journey offers Dickens the perfect opportunity to experiment, in the rather tight confines of a simple plot, with a diversity of character voices, almost all of them extreme— Oliver is extremely young and innocent, Mr. Bumble is extremely pompous, Mr. Brownlow is extremely benevolent,

Bill Sikes is extremely cruel, Fagin is extremely cunning—and with variety in the narrative voice.

Every novelist seeks, both consciously and unconsciously, to extend his range of expression. Dickens was especially energetic in seeking out dramatic incidents and unusual characters and new material; he also possessed a constitutional restlessness that brought him into contact with a range of classes and individuals almost uniquely broad. In his twenties, he was not unlike other youthful authors. Even though he was a genius, he had artistic ambitions that he was not yet technically equipped to fulfill, and he used his first three books to write his way toward fulfilling them. The *Sketches* expressed the plenitude of his interests but did not unify them. *Pickwick* gave voice to his very rich and ready comic sensibility but suffered from a certain bland digressiveness. *Oliver Twist* allowed him access to a wide variety of strong emotions, both through and about his characters and their world, but was too vividly colored and suffered from a lack of the very naturalness that the other books had possessed.

Nevertheless, between December 1, 1833, when his first piece ran in the *Monthly Magazine,* and November 9, 1838, when *Oliver Twist* was published in three volumes, Charles Dickens had become the most important literary figure of his day, the first Victorian novelist. Victoria herself was only newly crowned (as of January 1837). Novelists who were later to emerge as Dickens's contemporaries and rivals, such as William Makepeace Thackeray, Charlotte Brontë, and George Eliot, were still at home or in school. Even Elizabeth Gaskell, close in age to Dickens, hadn't begun to write. In a very real sense, he was in the process of creating the literary age that the others would be part of. He was so popular and so dominant a figure as both author and editor that the others would have to create their literary sensibilities more or less in reference to his.

But Charles Dickens was not only a famous author, he was also a self-conscious and responsible citizen, who never forgot that his fame gave him an unusual opportunity to comment upon and influence political events. Already by 1839, at the age of twenty-seven, Dickens was being honored by his friends for his active benevolence—Macready declared that Dickens "had made the amelioration of his fellow man the object of all his labors." Consciousness of the sufferings of the impoverished classes ran through all his activities, from the walks he took that carried him into every neighborhood, to the issues, such as the New Poor Law, that he wrote about, both in fiction and in his journalism, to the public speeches that he made and the fund-raisers that he organized to benefit fellow artists or their dependents.

Charity and charitable enterprises were at the very heart of Victorian life and constituted the main way in which those unable to take care of themselves were taken care of by society. Very few social services as we know them were provided by the government—rather, churches and privately supported charitable institutions, upholding a wide variety of theories and methods, provided education, sustenance, sometimes employment, and care for those in need. Dickens did not uniformly support all of these institutions, especially not those sponsored by Evangelical groups. The combination of puritanical narrowness and crabbed strictness opposed Dickens's instinctive sense that true charity was an outgrowth of kindly benevolence and good cheer. He had his own theories about the failures of his society and their proper alleviation, and he was frequently in sympathy with radical political ideas. At the same time, he deeply distrusted social unrest, including incipient revolutionary movements, labor strikes, or any potential violent confrontation between classes. Social order was his highest goal, a social order that recognized the responsibility of all to all and made plenty of room for the pleasures of life—entertainment, good fellowship, good food and drink, congenial surroundings, familial affection. While he feared social unrest, he deplored any means by which the moneyed classes might shirk their social responsibilities: harsh poor laws, legal obfuscation, bureaucratic incompetence and red tape, failure to attend to public works and public sanitation, or simple personal selfishness and profligacy. It can be fairly argued, in this context, that Dickens never shirked his. His mode of life demonstrated that he lived by play as well as work, believed equally in the value of each, and promoted the value of both for all members of Victorian society. In 1839, Dickens met Angela Burdett-Coutts, the heiress to the Coutts banking fortune, the wealthiest woman in England other than the queen. Two years younger than Dickens, Miss Coutts remained single until eleven years after Dickens's death and devoted herself to a wide range of charitable projects, in many of which Dickens was her partner and agent, especially a project for retraining and rehabilitating fallen women, called Urania Cottage.

From his earliest writings, Dickens frequently expressed the opinion that ignorance and want go hand in hand and together cause many social ills, from disease to crime to social unrest. Over and over, his depictions of children included critiques of cruel, ineffectual, and neglectful educational institutions, and he relentlessly made the point that the child is father to the man. In his third novel, *Nicholas Nickleby* (which began to appear at the end of March 1838), he succeeded in bringing together several of his concerns and several of his customary styles, and he produced what may be seen as his first wide-ranging "Dickensian" novel. Depiction of an educational institution—one of the "Yorkshire schools," where illegitimate and otherwise inconvenient children were warehoused at low cost by their families—was his avenue into the novel, but as yet he was not quite ready to form the entire narrative around a single overarching theme, as he was later to do with *Bleak House* and *Little Dorrit*. He took as his protagonist a young man not unlike himself or, perhaps, a young man who was a combination of himself and the standard hero of a melodrama. Nicholas's father dies of grief over losing his property, and Nicholas, his sister, Kate, and their mother go to London and seek the aid of their uncle, Ralph Nickleby. Ralph is a moneylender, a greedy, heartless rich man who has no family feeling other than a long-standing contemptuous envy for his more humane but less successful brother. Ralph and Nicholas are soon bitter enemies. Ralph consents to help Mrs. Nickleby and Kate on the condition that Nicholas accept employment with Squeers, the proprietor of one of the Yorkshire schools.

The plot of *Nicholas Nickleby* is episodic and owes a considerable amount to the devices of early Victorian drama—Ralph's villainy is unrelieved and relentless, and Nicholas's heart is invariably pure. It is the peripheral characters that Nicholas encounters as he makes his way who supply the humor and psychological interest. The young, romantic lead characters are not so idiosyncratic, and their dilemmas are rather formulaic. But *Nicholas Nickleby* is a lively and entertaining reading experience and, in the context of Dickens's other works, has several features of interest. Whereas the Pickwickians went out into the world to see what they might see, a leisure activity, and Oliver went out to find himself a home, Nicholas must confront the choices of a life work and a life partner (choices Dickens himself had had to make rather recently). He has to find a way to make himself an agent in the world rather than an observer, like the Pickwickians, but neither does he need or desire to escape the world, like Oliver; so Dickens has a look at several types of work—education, art, theater, finance, business, and fashionable dressmaking. There is even a portrayal of aristocratic profligacy as a career. Nicholas's story is the story of making choices, and therefore seeking maturity, though in the conventional modes of work and domestic life.

It is evident from the tone of the novel, which is ebullient and lively, that Dickens was enjoying his own domestic life (a few days before the publication of the novel in volume form, at the end of October 1839, Dickens and Catherine had a third child, Kate). The final image of *Nickleby* is of happy marital fertility—Nicholas and Madeline's children gathered about the quiet grave of Smike, honoring his memory. *Nickleby* is remarkable among Dickens's work for other reasons as well. Sir Mulberry Hawke and his associates are open sexual predators, who prey upon Kate with the collusion of her uncle, and, in a different way, the lascivious designs of the old miser, Gride, upon Madeline Bray are expressed and developed. In fact, much of the peril of Madeline's sacrificial marriage arises from the image of the young beautiful girl in the arms of the repulsive old man. *Nicholas Nickleby* is full of lusty men, young and old, and their beautiful objects of desire. In an interesting twist, Mr. Mantalini, who lives off his wife, repeatedly uses the language of ardent romance to woo her and blind her to the financial ruin he is bringing upon her establishment. This relative openness about romance and sexuality is not characteristic of later Dickens novels, which take a much less earthy view of happy domesticity and a much darker view of marriage in general. But the brightness of *Nickleby* is of its historical as well as its biographical moment—at the end of the 1830s, the respectability of Victorianism had not yet entirely supplanted the rowdiness of the eighteenth century, and traces of older ways remain in what we might otherwise see as the first truly characteristic novel of the most characteristic novelist of the Victorian period.

Nicholas Nickleby was successful as a serial publication, selling fifty thousand copies of the first number and maintaining sales throughout, then selling well as a volume, too. Its popularity did not sustain itself, however, and the novel became one of Dickens's least read works, a high-spirited but not quite successful transitional novel in which Dickens began to try out the ideas and methods that would bear fruit a few years later.

CHAPTER TWO

By 1838, the shape of Charles Dickens's life was firmly set. Its typical features were to remain unchanged thereafter for some eighteen years: celebrity, conviviality, restlessness, hard work, ambivalent domesticity, all forms of literary endeavor from the most private to the most public, and most forms of civic responsibility from private charity to public pronouncements.

Among Dickens's many friends was the artist and illustrator Daniel Maclise, who painted a portrait of Dickens while he was completing *Nicholas Nickleby* that now hangs in the National Portrait Gallery in London. The portrait was considered by Dickens's friends to be an excellent likeness. It was unveiled at a dinner held to celebrate the completion of *Nickleby* and was later engraved and included in the bound volumes of the novel as the frontispiece. Here is Charles Dickens at twenty-seven, the most famous writer of his day. He is turned to his left, and light from some source falls full on his face. His countenance is handsome and youthful, with a high forehead, large eyes, a prominent nose, and curving lips. Light also falls on his hands, one of which is splayed across the pages of a manuscript. The fingers are long and graceful. Dickens's hair is flowing and dark, he is clean-shaven, he is wearing a dark suit and a dark cravat at his neck. He looks pensive and "literary." He also looks extremely young, younger than his age, his experience, and the self-confident sophistication of his writing style. If, indeed, his friends considered it a proper likeness, then surely one thing they saw in it would have been its air of quietness almost unto sadness.

But even so, Dickens's more signal quality, the one most often commented upon by his acquaintances and the one he relied upon at all times, was his energy. It was in this period that he took up the habit of long, vigorous daily walks that seem almost unimaginable today for an otherwise very busy man with many obligations. At a pace of twelve to fifteen minutes per mile, he regularly covered twenty and sometimes thirty miles. Returning, as his brother-in-law said, "he looked the personification of energy, which seemed to ooze from every pore as from some hidden reservoir. . . ." His energy contended with discouragement, fear, discontent, and illness—he had been frequently ill as a child, and recurrent bouts of a painful kidney ailment, as well as some sort of facial neuralgia, nervous exhaustion, and various infectious diseases, continued to plague him. He veered between overflowing vitality and prostration in a manner that seems to the modern sensibility almost hysterical. Every stimulus produced an enormous reaction, to the point that right around this period in Dickens's life, it was rumored that he was mad. Certainly, he was frenzied, and certainly, in the grips of inspiration, he had only tenuous control over his facial expressions and his tongue. His daughter Kate as an adult recalled watching Dickens at work; the characters and their voices seemed to possess him—he spoke their lines and acted out their parts as he wrote them down, often looking into a mirror.

In the first five years of their marriage, Charles and Catherine produced four children and officially moved their household three times, but additionally, each summer they moved to various rented houses at Broadstairs, or Petersham, in Kent, and back to London in the autumn. They traveled abroad as well, to France, Belgium, and the Isle of Wight. That this restlessness was stressful to the marriage cannot be doubted—Dickens's letters increasingly betray dissatisfaction with Catherine's "slowness" and her invariable postpartum depressions. It seems not to have occurred to him that curbing his own appetites and relieving her from an endless cycle of pregnancy and parturition was a possibility. Rather he looked to her, or to her doctors, to strengthen her and fortify her capacity to live up to the image he had of what his wife should be and do. His sense of grief and loss over the death of Catherine's sister Mary remained powerful and overt, and possibly distressing, to Catherine, but he showed no awareness, once again, that his behavior needed modifying. There is also no doubt that Dickens had strict and rigorous views about how the household was to be run. He expected absolute order and meticulous cleanliness, quiet when he was working, and boisterous fun, with many visitors, when he was ready for it. He was, in short, something of a domestic tyrant, whose sensitivity to the needs of his wife (toward whom he still seems to have felt considerable affection at this point) and children (in whose lives he always interfered) was minimal.

Nor was his professional life peaceful. Dickens's entire career was marked by deals made in great jubilation and rather soon broken off in anger and enmity. There were, of course, always circumstances and issues. In the case of *Bentley's Miscellany*, which Dickens was editing and where *Oliver Twist* had appeared, Dickens was annoyed when Richard Bentley, the magazine's owner and publisher, inserted some pieces in the September 1837 number on his own. More important was Dickens's feeling that he had not been paid enough for *Oliver Twist*, a feeling that intensified and, ultimately, led to a serious dispute after *Oliver Twist* became enormously popular; yet Bentley failed to offer more lucrative terms for *Barnaby Rudge*, the second novel in the contract Dickens had with him. Dickens's sense of his own popularity and earning potential was now considerably changed from 1836, when he first went to work for Bentley. He was no longer "primus inter pares" among a group of authors. He was a star, *the* star. The legality or morality of contractual agreements had to give way, and give way it did. Dickens had already found more congenial publishers in the firm of Chapman and Hall, who had published *The Pickwick Papers* and *Nicholas Nickleby* and were careful (under the urging of John Forster, who served as Dickens's business agent) to be liberal both in their remuneration and in the flexibility of their contract terms. Dickens was beginning to feel, with justification, that anything he might choose to do would be popular and lucrative, and he was impatient for the freedom to do it.

The fact was, though, that Dickens's work, career, and domestic life were bound together in a tight knot not easily unraveled by anything as clear as contractual obligations. When the subject was money, there could be no uncomplicated thoughts or feelings for Charles Dickens. Money—what could be earned, how it would be spent, what it meant, its effects on a man's or woman's character and fate, whether and how it would be given away—was a subject that obsessed Dickens for his entire life and, it may be said, finally killed him. The deals he made and broke over the years were only the most straightforward symptom of the whole tangle.

If we see Dickens as the first true celebrity of the popular arts—that is, a man whose work made him rich and widely famous, as close to a household name as any movie star is today—then we also can see him as the first person to become a "name brand." For many years, his name on the first installment of a serialization sold copies in and of itself. By the third or fourth installment, sales would have either climbed or dropped off (in which case Dickens would modify his plan to bolster them), but he counted on his name to bring in a certain number of readers, and he felt a strong obligation toward them. He always felt his job was to please and entertain readers, not to shock and confront them, and certainly not to offend them. Unlike writers such as Thackeray and Bulwer-Lytton, Dickens's contemporaries and friends, he had no resources of family money or land to fall back upon; and unlike, say, Charlotte Brontë, he had no desire to live a modest or retiring life. He put his faith in hard work, and in hard work that would always be tremendously successful. His financial obligations left little leeway for the natural ebb and flow of audience loyalty or the vagaries of artistic experimentation. His convivial temperament expressed itself in a natural love of display—he was a snappy dresser (a little flamboyant, according to most of his contemporaries), and few of the joys and pleasures of life that he cherished were ascetic ones. He was generous and hospitable, for the most part, though he had a streak of frugality that some of his family might have considered to be miserly. The fact was, he had an ever growing set of dependents, not only his wife and children and household servants, but also his parents and, from time to time, his brothers. He tried to live out the earthly paradise that his books so frequently depicted—fecundity and domestic peace, liberality and comfort, freedom and safety. Such things were not only images that appeared in his writings, but also principles and personal aspirations. What is important to remember about them, however, was that they had their entire source in his own sense of himself. As much as any public figure of his time, Charles Dickens was more than a self-made man, he was a self-made phenomenon—he generated out of his own being all the energy and imagination to both envision his goal and get himself to it. His particular visionary literary style not only found favor with Victorian audiences, it defined for them the world that they inhabited, not only as it was but as it could be.

At the same time, there is never as much money to be made in art, no matter how popular, as there is in manufacture or speculation. The machinery of composition never powers itself, but instead draws more and more deeply upon the inventiveness and the astuteness of the artist. An artist who relies, as Dickens did, upon always outdoing himself in order to pay for obligations already contracted and habits already formed inevitably feels pressed for money and is always underestimating the creative cost of adding one more endeavor.

In his late twenties, though, the readiness of Dickens's response to the creative demands of the moment was astounding. His first notion of the publication he was going to produce for Chapman and Hall was a weekly periodical to be called *Master Humphrey's Clock*. The conceit would be of a small group of retiring men, friends of "Master Humphrey," who would find in his old grandfather clock "sketches, essays, tales, adventures, letters from imaginary correspondents, and so forth." The model was to be eighteenth-century journals such as *The Spectator*. Dickens began to serialize *The Old Curiosity Shop* in the first week of April 1840. The first issue sold well, but not the next few, and it was clear that the original concept left something to be desired. Dickens's response was to expand upon what had been a freestanding sketch concerning Nell, Kit Nubbles, and the grandfather's shop, told by Master Humphrey. In a few weeks, all of Master Humphrey and his friends had dropped away, and the weekly journal consisted entirely of the serialization of Nell's story. Commercially, Dickens's story performed exactly as he hoped—it was an enormous success. It was published in weekly installments, which were gathered and republished in monthly installments, and at the end it was published in volume form. It sold over a hundred thousand copies per week, better than any previous Dickens novel, in some sense anticipating that phenomenon of the late twentieth century, the popular weekly television series. That American dockworkers met the ship carrying the installment wherein Nell died with shouts of "Is Nell still alive?" may be only a legend, but even so, the novel was hugely successful on both sides of the Atlantic.

Although he had miscalculated the costs of the handsome weekly numbers, thereby reducing his profits to some degree, Dickens himself was very pleased with the novel and wrote in March 1841 (around the time of completion) that he expected to always like it best. Certainly he was deeply involved with Nell and deeply affected by her death.

The Old Curiosity Shop was in Dickens's *Oliver Twist* mode rather than his *Nicholas Nickleby* mode. As in *Oliver Twist,* his protagonist is an innocent child lost in one of the crueler byways of adult commerce, beset by human predators whose features are both mechanical and demonic. Those whose job it is to protect her are powerless to do so. The villain of the novel, the dwarf moneylender Daniel Quilp, gains control of Nell and her grandfather through the grandfather's attempts to win sustenance for Nell by gambling. In a related plot, Dick Swiveller, a young law clerk who is covetous of Nell, is redeemed through coming to understand the true nature of his employers, Sampson Brass and his sister Sally, and through the love of their oppressed maidservant. Kit finds marital redemption, but Nell dies, pure and uncorrupted.

The Old Curiosity Shop is Dickens's most interesting novel in terms of the extremes of reaction it elicits in readers. Legendarily popular and lucrative in its day, it is now impossible for many to read, even those who are devoted Dickensians. Oscar Wilde remarked, "One must have a heart of stone to read the death of Nell without laughing," and others have been at least as critical. The kindest thing most modern readers think of it is that it vividly shows the differences between the sensibility of the mid-nineteenth century and our own.

Critics and social historians point out that the progress of the nineteenth century on both sides of the Atlantic was marked by the steadily increasing suppression of public displays of emotion among men, as the image of proper manhood was modified by the influences of colonialism, industrialism, militarism, and financial speculation. After the marriage of Victoria and Albert, in 1840, gender roles became more sharply divided, with women exaggerating the putative qualities of femininity (privacy, tender feeling, fragility) and men the putative qualities of masculinity (public action, stoicism, strength). The theory goes that the effect of *The Old Curiosity Shop*, which relies upon the reader's readiness to feel the extreme pathos of the sufferings and innocence of Little Nell, would be blunted for the post-Victorian reader, who filters his or her sense of pathos through more layers of irony than Dickens's contemporaries did.

The Old Curiosity Shop defines an outer boundary of one of Dickens's modes of imagining his world, and it is a world peopled by unrealistic, fairy-tale figures of ogres and princesses and fools. Dickens often told his friends that he had loved fairy tales as a child and that he still approved of them as an adult for their antidote to the dead, commercial, mechanical life that seemed to be taking over all around him. Among the many risks Dickens takes in *The Old Curiosity Shop* is setting the stark fairy-tale world of Nell and her grandfather right next to the somewhat more comic and realistic world of Dick Swiveller. Nell's life-and-death journey continually breaks into and overwhelms the much less desperate psychological journey that Dick takes, but they are meant to coexist and to comment on each other, mimicking the ways in which different lives have different tonal and mythic qualities. That Dickens can't quite balance them at this point in his career is not especially surprising. In part we see the temptation and the pressure of improvisation—Dickens was writing in short weekly parts, and he was acutely aware of what the selling points of the serial were. The novel surely felt like a high-wire act that was succeeding magnificently, encouraging him to write from instinct even more than he had in the past. Nell's fate also certainly drew upon his still fresh sense of grief at the death of Mary Hogarth.

Dickens's own sense of pleasure and accomplishment at the completion of the novel indicates that its extremes felt right to him and that its sales proved to him that they were right in fact. The tone of the novel is almost a denial of the tone of *Nickleby*, with its broad and cheery qualities. Certain *Nickleby* figures return, especially the figure of the money-lender, but now the recognizably human Ralph Nickleby (who even has a few softer notions and second thoughts) has become Daniel Quilp, deformed and inhuman, a monster with a sense of wit and huge energy. Nell herself is similar to the young women in *Nickleby*, in that she must go into the world unprotected, but now her very purity forbids contact with it—there is no young man, like Nicholas, pure enough to protect her, and death is the only option.

Without engaging in excessive Freudian second-guessing of the author, it is interesting to accept the invitation offered by the quickness and ease of the novel's gestation, and ask what light it sheds upon Dickens's sense of himself and of his life's possibilities at this point, a time when to all appearances he was hugely successful. Clearly, he saw innocence itself as something possessed in its purest form by certain presexual women. The ideal of domesticity that he had written about and attempted to live now came second, morally, and was good enough for the redeemed (Dick and Kit), but not for those who had never fallen (Nell). Nell's particular brand of innocence had specific qualities—endurance, forgiveness, martyrdom—that were to be seen in contrast with the dark, manic forces all around it. Quilp is not the only frenzied character—to a greater or lesser degree, the contrast between all of the other characters and Nell is in their greater expression of liveliness, or life. It is as if Nell must die because the energy of life is in itself tainted and destructive. Every novel is a logical argument—an assertion of the author's sense of what life is, embodied in characters, plots, and images. Some of these arguments have wide appeal, some don't; some have an appeal bolstered by intense emotional energy, some appeal essentially to reason and shared experience. The argument of *The Old Curiosity Shop* strikes many readers as a strange and unbelievable one.

On June 19, 1841, the Dickenses took a trip to Scotland. The high point, and a turning point in Dickens's sense of his own position in public life, came in Edinburgh on June 25, when the city threw for him a public dinner, a sort of occasion unfamiliar to us, but rather like a cross between the Academy Awards and getting the key to the city. Weekly serialization of *The Old Curiosity Shop* had given way, in the late winter, to weekly serialization of *Barnaby Rudge,* which was also quite popular. Walter, child number four and boy number two, had been born in February, the day after Dickens's twenty-ninth birthday. Dickens was used to fame, adulation, and importance, but somehow this public dinner, with 250 male guests eating and 200 women coming in after dinner to listen to the speeches from galleries above, impressed upon him that he was more than famous and more than a literary man, but something on the order of a national treasure (if it is possible for someone to think of himself as such a thing). He had achieved not simply literary success, but something else, a separate status. His voice and his vision had become *beloved;* as Ackroyd puts it, he was "public property." His first reaction was very typical of the public Dickens—when he stood to make his own speech, he was poised, articulate, modest, cool, and, most of all, charming. When he later wrote to Forster about it, the tone of his letter was exultant, pleased, and, at least to some degree, amazed. He seems to have been especially struck by the fact that he was so young and the men who came to celebrate him were old and established.

In his *Charles Dickens: A Literary Life,* Grahame Smith points out that in the twelve years between the publication of Sir Walter Scott's last book, *Redgauntlet,* and the publication of *The Pickwick Papers,* novel writing in England had been going through something of a lull. Publishing itself changed in those twelve years, as periodicals found their way to a more numerous and socially broader audience, taking their place beside the expensively bound three-volume novel, which cost just over a pound and a half, equivalent to something like $52 today. The Romantic period was long over, and the Victorian era had not begun. Interesting novels were being published in France by Balzac, Stendhal, and others, and in the United States by Washington Irving, but in England only Tennyson's lyrics, De Quincey's memoirs, and Carlyle's *Sartor Resartus* were of any note. When Chapman and Hall began publishing the novels of Charles Dickens, the idea that a company would publish only books and profit from them, rather than printing books and newspapers and selling them along with stationery, was a very new one.

The new thing, in every way, was for an author to support himself or herself through sales of his or her work, and in this Dickens was pioneer and exemplar. The form of serial monthly or weekly publication not only helped him find a wide audience (every issue sold, it has been estimated, found fifteen readers), it also helped him keep that audience interested. The analogy, of course, is to weekly television or soap opera–type serials. Dickens's exquisite natural responsiveness, combined with his amazing inventiveness, meant that a form other authors found onerous was perfectly suited to him.

Another thing that made Dickens a national treasure, though, had nothing to do with publishing and everything to do with Dickens's class origins or, rather, the fluidity of his class origins. Carried upward and downward by the vagaries of his father's career and poor money management, and then by his own hard work and genius, Dickens found himself in a unique position to observe all facets of English society. He was unconstrained by a classical education, untrained, as it were, to look at English society in the traditional way. His first thirty years were, in a fashion that contrasted with that of almost everyone around him, a training in freedom—in forming his own opinions, in judging for himself, in observing the effects of one group upon another, one class upon another, of institutions upon individuals and individuals upon institutions. He differed from all of his contemporaries in that he represented no group, therefore he came to represent all. His medium, the novel, enhanced his freedom, since the novel can never work except through freedom—the author is free to write, and the reader is free to read. Dickens understood as well as anyone ever that the reader can always close the cover, and his art always responded to the fact that the reader can choose to buy or not to buy the next number. The very oddities of both the man and his work further promoted his freedom, since his mind ranged freely over all sorts of characters, ideas, and settings. And he frequently took pains to speak out against abridgments of freedom, such as the closing of shops on Sunday, the only day when working people were able to buy, and other laws restricting the lives of the poor, as well as narrow and joyless religious and charitable institutions. By temperament, by training, and by intention, Dickens was a modern man, whose essential quality was the desire for freedom of thought and action.

The lull in the production of English novels between 1824 and 1836 marks the birth of modernity. Austen and Scott, whose novels are set in the countryside, give way to Dickens, a man of the city. The tissue of relationships and obligations that mark traditional society give way to the casual meetings and commercial connections that mark modern society. For me, the moment where literature enters the modern world is very particular. In Nikolai Gogol's story "The Nose," published in *St. Petersburg Stories* in 1835, the protagonist searches all over St. Petersburg for his vagrant nose. He pauses in his search to look at an advertisement in a shop window for ladies' stockings. He is struck by the picture of the woman's leg slipping into the stocking. He moves on, but he has just had a thoroughly modern moment—sex and graphics have combined to turn him into a potential customer. The other features of modernity—rapid transportation, industrial production, financial speculation, the wholesale dissemination of information, the rise of the middle class, the elevation of materialism, general education—all of these are still to come, but advertising is the singing canary, alerting us to what is in store. The power of advertising and its capacity to connect him to and enlarge his audience was something Dickens comprehended at once and completely. He was at home in his milieu.

Dickens in Edinburgh in the middle of his thirtieth year is an original without a progenitor. Most other great innovators owe something to someone—even Shakespeare was preceded by Christopher Marlowe, and he did not create the theaters in which his plays were performed or the companies that performed them. Dickens, however, spoke in a new voice, in a new form, to a new audience, of a new world, about several old ideas reconsidered for the new system of capitalism—that care and respect are owed to the weakest and meekest in society, rather than to the strongest; that the ways in which class and money divide humans from one another are artificial and dangerous; that pleasure and physical comfort are positive goods; that the spiritual lives of the powerful have social and economic ramifications. We might today call this an ecological perspective, an intuitive understanding of the social world as a web rather than a hierarchy—the quintessential modern mode of seeing the world. Dickens grasped this idea from the earliest stages of his career and demonstrated his increasingly sophisticated grasp of it in the plots, characterizations, themes, and style of every single novel he wrote. This is the root source of his greatness. That he did so in English at the very moment when England was establishing herself as a worldwide force is the root source of his importance. That he combined his artistic vision with social action in an outpouring of energy and hard work is the root source of his uniqueness.

Charles and Catherine returned to London from Scotland in mid-July, then went to Broadstairs in Kent for the rest of the summer. Dickens had begun to think of traveling to the United States, no doubt encouraged by a letter from Washington Irving, who promised, in the wake of the success of *The Old Curiosity Shop,* that a Dickens tour of America would be an unprecedented triumph— and certainly for Dickens this meant not only fame, but money. In addition, the themes of *Barnaby Rudge,* which takes place during the American Revolutionary era, had inflamed his desire to see the land of newness for himself. Notes and memoirs by European travelers to America abounded in the 1830s and 1840s—it was practically a cottage industry, and surely Dickens knew that he had something original to contribute. He broached the topic to his friend Forster in mid-September and had already made up his mind a week later. Unfortunately, Catherine, mother of four, including a seven-month-old baby, did not want to go. Ackroyd notes that she wept every time he mentioned his plans, but as usual, he was not to be denied, and within weeks plans for the journey, to be made by steamship (and the first steamship had crossed the Atlantic only four years before), were in full swing. Of course, it was to be a lengthy journey, almost six months, and the children were to be left behind in the care of Dickens's brother Fred. Dickens was undaunted, as well, by an operation he elected to undergo in the autumn—the repair of a fistula in his rectal wall, without anesthetic, so painful in the retelling, according to his friend Macready, that Macready could hardly force himself to sit still to listen to Dickens's recounting it. Nevertheless, Dickens completed the last installments of *Barnaby Rudge* while recuperating.

On January 2, Charles and Catherine boarded the *Britannia* and set sail for America. The journey was not quite as it had been advertised—the couple's stateroom was so tiny that he likened stowing their trunks to forcing a giraffe into a flowerpot. But he took his usual lively interest in everything there was to see, writing later in *American Notes* that "one party of men were 'taking in the milk,' or, in other words, getting the cow on board; and another were filling the ice-houses to the very throat with fresh provisions; with butcher's meat and garden stuff, pale sucking pigs, calves' heads in scores, beef, veal, and pork, and poultry out of all proportion. . . ." The captain later arrived in a small boat, and he was just what Dickens hoped for, "a well-made, tight-built, dapper little fellow; with a ruddy face, which is a letter of invitation to shake him by both hands at once, and a clear blue, honest eye that it does one good to see one's sparkling image in." What boded well did not go well—the eighteen-day journey was an arduous labor of heavy seas, dazed seasickness, cold, and fear. Even so, even though both Charles and Catherine were nearly overcome by anxiety, Dickens, as always, was able to enjoy certain things and to evoke them for his readers—after days at sea, he writes, "the captain (who never goes to bed and is never out of humor) turns up his coat collar for the deck again; shakes hands all around; and goes laughing out into the weather as merrily as to a birthday party."

Dickens was thrilled to get to America, and not only to terra firma. His popularity there, combined with his critique of English society, had convinced him that he and the citizens of the United States would feel an instant and abiding sense of kinship and would recognize themselves in each other. There was also an assumption on both sides that too much celebrity was not possible—the Americans had prepared to make the most of Dickens's visit, with balls and parties and receptions and every sort of opportunity to view the author. Dickens, used to fame of a familiar sort, public events interspersed with private time to work and spend with his family, was unprepared for what was expected of him (though it looks perfectly familiar to us). In Boston, Hartford, New Haven, New York, and Philadelphia, there were just too many occasions, too many expectations, and Dickens's mood soured. We can recognize it as a nightmare book tour, the author and his wife unprotected by publicists or any sort of previous experience. All the features of modern American celebrity leap forth, full grown—the public's sense that they have the right to gaze upon the Dickenses at will, the gossip in the press about their every characteristic, the sense the Dickenses have of being objectified and hounded and intruded upon, the resentment of the public at any sort of behavior on the part of the author other than gratitude and good cheer, and, above all, the assumption that all fame, all the time, must be a good thing.

Dickens quickly offended his hosts. He had not reckoned with the New England conservatism and provincial snobbishness of those he met in Boston, who were eager to see his mode of dressing and speaking as evidence of ungentlemanly origins. He was short, he had big ears, he talked quickly—he was not the titan Americans expected. In addition, he mentioned several times his indignation that American newspapers and periodicals were in the habit of reprinting his works without paying for them, that this was, in fact, standard publishing procedure. Over this issue, he did something that every media-savvy man or woman knows, after fifty years of television, is exactly the wrong thing to do—he lost his temper. The response in the press was immediate and, to us, predictable. He was attacked, denigrated, ridiculed. Everyone, including Dickens, realized at once and completely that Dickens was an Englishman, with characteristic English ways of doing and perceiving things, and more important, that he was a man and not an ideal figure, not the amazing, soothing, genial, and visionary voice of the narrators of his books, coming into the home with every new number of each novel, taking his place at the fireside and in the reader's consciousness, but a specific male human being, not always lovable or wise or admirable. Thus the perennial disappointment of celebrity was played out at once, with the first great media celebrity. His works had made promises of a personal nature that the man himself was bound to renege upon, no matter how much energy and goodwill he possessed.

In addition, while the purpose of Dickens's trip, to the Americans, was to be looked at, for Dickens, it was to look—like other European travelers, he wanted to see what there was to see, and he had a particular interest in social institutions. He had criticized England for the piecemeal and often cruel ways in which the least fortunate members of society were cared for, so in America he was interested in orphanages, and schools, and prisons, and factories. He toured any number of them and, overall, was impressed, especially by the factory systems of such towns as Lowell, Massachusetts, where the working girls were regulated and given decent wages and places to live, as well as certain freedoms. He made friends, some of whom he corresponded with for the rest of his life. Notable among these was Cornelius Felton, a self-made scholar of humble origins, who taught Greek at Harvard and was not the sort of man Dickens could have come to know at an English university. He visited the South—Washington, Baltimore, and Richmond, Virginia—but was uncomfortable there with what he saw as the negative effects of slavery, both on the inhabitants and on the ambience of the city. He liked Cincinnati, did not like St. Louis, hated the southern Illinois reaches of the Mississippi River, disliked the roughness and danger of riverboat travel (though he pursued his walking regime with great energy when traveling by canal boat).

Catherine was a patient and submissive companion and in fact made a better impression upon the Americans than Dickens himself did. He complained about her once, that she could not get into or out of any conveyance without stumbling, but in general he recognized the sacrifices she was daily making to accompany him on a journey that she had never wanted to take. They seemed to be well matched and happily married to those who witnessed them, and he seemed, in his letters to friends, to be pleased with her. They were equal in their hunger to hear from home and, as the end of the journey neared, to get home.

At Niagara Falls, for once, Dickens's expectations were more than fulfilled. He looked upon the "fall of bright green water" and "then, when I felt how near to my Creator I was standing, the first effect, and the enduring one—instant and lasting—of the tremendous spectacle was Peace. Peace of mind, tranquillity, calm recollections of the Dead, great thoughts of Eternal Rest and Happiness: nothing of gloom or terror. Niagara was at once stamped upon my heart, an Image of Beauty; to remain there, changeless and indelible, until its pulses cease to beat forever." They remained on the Canadian side for ten days, vacationing, enjoying the falls from every angle, shunning company (the Canadian side was less inhabited), and renewing themselves. Thus refreshed, they went on to Toronto, Montreal, and Quebec, where they had a better time—in Montreal, in fact, both Charles and Catherine acted in a theatrical production of several short plays, something Dickens hadn't done in years and enjoyed very much (he was also a great success).

They were more than eager to get home. On the seventh of June, he writes, he "darted out of bed" at dawn to check the wind (they were sailing rather than steaming home), and on the first of July they arrived. Of their homecoming, Dickens writes, "The country, by the railroad, seemed, as we rattled through it, like a luxuriant garden. The beauty of the fields (so small they looked!), the hedgerows, and the trees; the pretty cottages, the beds of flowers, the old churchyards, and antique houses, and every well-known object; the exquisite delights of that one journey crowding, in the short compass of a summer's day, the joy of many years. . . ."

If much of Dickens's life seems emblematically Victorian to us, of more than historical interest only in the light of his literary genius, this American trip, by contrast, seems uncannily modern. The new machinery of capitalistic publishing had carried his work far and wide, bringing a single man, a single voice, into a personal relationship with huge numbers of people whom he had never met, and yet who felt intimate with him, because the novel is, above all, an intense experience of prolonged intimacy with another consciousness. But both the author and the readers had misread the relationship. The readers had mistaken the work for the man; the man had mixed fame and money together without realizing that they were distinct compensations that did not necessarily overlap. The intimacy they felt through the work came from the natural power of the novel to cross the boundaries of appearance and reveal the inner life, emphasizing the inner life in a delightful and, in a sense, false contrast to social life. This was the first time, but it had all the qualities of the countless similar episodes to take place between then and now, whether the art form in question is novel writing or moviemaking or television broadcasting. And then, the couple's return is familiar, too, to anyone who has ever traveled from America to England—the loveliness, the tidiness, the gardenlike contrast to the rougher, vaster, less inhabited continent to the west.

Tastes differ. Many of us discover a deep attachment to the unpredictability of America—Dickens discovered an attachment to the very circumscriptions, of fields, of villages, of private life, of the England wherein he had never before quite consciously felt at home.

Dickens was eager to go to work. He commenced immediately upon *American Notes for General Circulation,* moved the family to Broadstairs for the rest of the summer, and adopted into the household as a permanent addition Georgina Hogarth, Catherine's fourteen-year-old sister, who had been helping Fred Dickens with the children while Charles and Catherine were away. Georgina reminded Dickens of Mary, and he became very fond of her over the next years, installing her as the children's general caretaker and governess.

American Notes was written quickly, largely because Dickens could refer to all the letters he had written Forster from abroad. He originally wrote a strongly hostile introduction, which Forster persuaded him to drop. The volume was published in October, only three and a half months after his return. Reviews and sales in England were disappointing—he had not had as much to say of interest as his public expected. Reviews in America were angry, but sales were good. Unfortunately, owing to the very copyright questions that had been at issue while he was there, he earned nothing from them. Nevertheless, in contrast with the many other travel narratives of the time, *American Notes* does now seem "Dickensian." While the style does not have the density and power of his best work, it is lively, witty, and intelligent, and the author discusses typical subjects for him—prisons and other public institutions, odd characters and odd characteristics. Dickens was possessed of tremendous powers of observation, greater than those of any other writer. *American Notes* stands out from other books of its kind for these qualities of precise notice. He did not, however, have the same sort of distilled and profound understanding of American institutions and the American landscape that he had for England and, subsequently, for France and Italy. Nor did he have the love for the place and the leisure it would have taken to develop a vital relationship with the United States. That the journey was a tiresome disappointment in many ways is evident in the volume's lack of real power. It was only subsequently, in *Martin Chuzzlewit,* that Dickens managed to incorporate America into his inner world and give it his characteristic qualities and symbolic force.

It is clear that upon his return from America, Dickens's sense of what he wanted to do in his work enlarged considerably, along with his sense of social responsibility. As soon as *American Notes* saw publication, he was off to Cornwall to have a look at the tin mines, as he had had a look at schools for *Nicholas Nickleby.* The contrasts he found between the United States and England did not all redound to the credit of the English—many social institutions, especially in New England, did a better and more complete job of taking care of citizens, especially indigent ones, than their English counterparts. Ackroyd is worth quoting on the state of London in the 1840s—indeed, almost throughout Dickens's life:

For most of his life Dickens lived in a city in which the odour of the dead emanated from metropolitan graveyards, where adults and children died of malnutrition or disease, where open sewers and cesspools spread their miasma into the foggy air, where it took only the shortest period to turn off one of the grand thoroughfares or respectable streets of the city and enter a landscape of filth, destitution, death, and misery. We have here glimpses of an urban life which is so alien to us as to seem almost incredible; but which for Dickens and his contemporaries was both common and familiar.

Just to make the point, let me add, "Burial grounds in the city . . . were now overflowing . . . the bodies were piled high upon each other, sometimes breaking through the soil and emitting noxious gases which poisoned and killed those in the vicinity." Ackroyd quotes one gravedigger: "I have been up to my knees in human flesh by jumping on the bodies so as to cram them into the least possible space at the bottom of the graves in which fresh bodies were afterwards placed."

Dickens, of course, was as familiar with such sordid scenes as any other Victorian, given his habit of perambulating the streets by night and day and his readiness to go anywhere and everywhere. Perhaps the London of his day is more analogous to the Mexico City or the Calcutta of our day than to any city in Europe or North America. Certainly an impoverished population was pouring into London all through the 1840s—there was a net increase of population of 250,000, in a time when the average life span of a Londoner was twenty-seven and almost half of all deaths were of children under the age of ten. Rather as Harriet Beecher Stowe was criticized in America for exaggerating the abuses of slavery when actually she tried to mitigate them in order to make reading about them palatable to her readers, Dickens saw and knew far more than he wrote of, simply because he always chose to appeal to rather than to confront his readers. His famous wish not to "bring a blush to the cheek of the young person" applied to the horror of social conditions as well as to sexual matters. Nevertheless, both as a social reformer and as a writer, the Dickens of late 1842 was more ambitious than the Dickens of 1841.

After completing *American Notes,* he was delayed for a bit casting about for the right name and title for his next serial. He tried Chuzzlewig, Sweezleden, Chuzzletoc, Sweezlebach, Sweezlewag. Chuzzlewit was it—the rightness of the name calling forth everything else, rather in the way Sir Laurence Olivier once said that putting on a false nose opened up everything else about a character for him. Dickens kept lists of names, noticed names in graveyards and newspapers. He was careful to name everything, including the periodicals he founded, before attempting anything further. That the names he chose were strange and evocative makes it all the more fascinating that many of the oddest ones, like "Flite" and "Guppy," were actual names of individuals.

Martin Chuzzlewit was the first of Dickens's novels to be written around an overriding idea—in this case the forms and effects of selfishness—and so marks a departure from the more personal and character-driven novels of his earlier period. In *Pickwick* and *Nickleby,* the eponymous heroes had gotten around quite a bit, and their travels had brought them into contact with various examples of human folly and knavery. Oliver and Nell, too, had embarked upon dark, and then darker, journeys. But the progress of each character toward his or her individual fate was paramount. Episodes and adventures and strange encounters could be a little arbitrary. The American journey had given Dickens many more specific opinions about himself and his society; more important, it had given him a vision that was more of a piece. When he arrived back in England on that first day, and saw everything rather smaller and more connected, it was as if it could be encompassed somehow, and understood, and, indeed, fixed. The reforming impulse begins, perhaps, in criticisms of society, but it relies upon the faith that what is wrong is only somewhat wrong—some money here, some effort there, some changes somewhere else, and the structure will yield to improvement. Additionally, improvements in the structure, be they sanitation, education, election reforms, or whatever, will produce better, more enlightened citizens, who will behave in a more community-minded fashion, turning away from evil and crime. In other words, human nature, too, is only somewhat wrong, not irredeemably corrupt and sinful. In this, Dickens differed from many of his fellow reformers, like Lord Shaftesbury, who were Evangelicals and promoted, first and foremost, the prohibition of sinful acts such as prostitution and alcohol consumption, who combined teaching the poor to read and write with rigorous religious instruction. Both sorts of reformers saw the inhumanity and, indeed, danger of the social chaos all around them, but Dickens always ridiculed the Evangelical impulse to look for sinfulness and evil nature, instead interpreting kindness, fellow-feeling, charitableness, and social conscience as virtues of generosity and love. Society would be reformed through an expansion of love and responsibility, through the cultivation of comfort and beauty, not through a clamping down. With *Martin Chuzzlewit,* he was beginning to grope toward a theory of how human networks function. Social ills still had their source in personal qualities—selfishness, for example—but he was now interested in the social ramifications of this single quality.

And everything went wonderfully. Evidence from the manuscript and the notes shows that he set about writing the first numbers more carefully than any previous serial, and evidence from letters shows that he was quite pleased with the results, especially with Pecksniff and Tom Pinch. In the meantime, his intimacy with Angela Burdett-Coutts was growing. She had the purse and he had the energy and the mobility to serve as her agent.

He first acted for her in investigating what were known as "ragged schools"—that is, charity schools for the very poorest children. While working on *Martin Chuzzlewit,* he took time to visit the Field Lane School in Saffron Hill, to report on conditions there and to suggest ways in which Miss Coutts might help. Saffron Hill was widely considered to be one of the very worst "rookeries," or slums, and coincidentally was familiar to Dickens from the *Oliver Twist* days. He remarked that the school was just where he had set Fagin's establishment. The condition of the children appalled him when he first visited—the stench was so great that his companion had to leave, and his very foremost recommendation to Miss Coutts was that the children be given a place to wash. Better ventilation, a larger space—there were certain basic changes that could be made, but in the absence of any sort of welfare structure or, indeed, any general social belief in what we might call the obligations of the state to care for its citizens, even the depth of Miss Coutts's purse was insignificant. Dickens was ambivalent about the ragged schools, feeling that they were not good schools in general and that the structure for educating the teachers was sadly wanting. He was hardly able even to name what we can readily see was a failure of the entire system, reflecting a wholesale shift in the social structure of England from rural to urban, from traditional to capitalistic, from patriarchal to democratic. But one thing to be said for Charles Dickens was that he remained undaunted. The energy he expended for Miss Coutts, the example he set in his public speeches, and the ambition of his novels steadily expanded.

Nevertheless, his ambitions were not immediately rewarded. Sales of *Martin Chuzzlewit* fell off almost at once. A hundred thousand copies of *The Old Curiosity Shop* had dwindled to twenty thousand copies of the new novel, and the terms of his contract meant that he had to pay back a portion of his advance if sales fell below a certain level. He was in debt to Chapman and Hall, *American Notes* had not done well, and his obligations were greater than ever. Not only was his household growing, his father and brothers were clamoring for assistance. In some sense, he had wasted his moment; instead of following *Barnaby Rudge* with a surefire repeat of "Dickensian" forms and themes, he had gone to America on an expensive trip that would not, owing to American copyright piracy, repay itself in sales. Dickens was enraged by the idea that he might have to fulfill the letter of his contract and make the payments to Chapman and Hall—he declared that he would write nothing for them ever again. As earlier, with

Bentley, he was ready and even eager to feel himself ill used by his publishers, as, truly, he *was* ill used by the Americans. Sales did not pick up. It is possible that a general business slowdown was the main cause. At any rate, Dickens decided that he could have it both ways—not only a strong overarching structure, but a bit of improvisation as well—and he sent Martin and his henchman, Mark Tapley, to America to seek their fortune, which they certainly did not find. Nor did the American chapters provide the sales boost Dickens hoped for. In the end, *Martin Chuzzlewit* turned out to be something of a commercial failure and got mixed reviews.

It is not uncommon, though, for a novelist to lose part of his audience as he grows more ambitious. The willingness, and maybe even the ability, of the audience to follow a favorite writer into work of greater complexity and more somber vision isn't always immediate, and every author whose sole income is from his writings has to reckon with this dilemma. Dickens had experienced the freedom, importance, and warm regard that come with great popularity; now he was discovering that the freedom was not absolute, and that the potential for corruption exists in artistic support through sales as well as through patronage. In our day, for example, the disinterested "patronage" of the university and the National Endowment for the Arts is attacked by conservatives who always assert that the marketplace is the best test of artistic value. It seems clear, though, from the history of novel writing since Dickens's time, that the production of enduring literary art has little or no relationship to market success, except insofar as a publisher can fund the publication of more complex and difficult works with the profits of a steady stream of popular stories. Even the most "loyal" readers grow "disloyal" when the work fails to please them.

But Dickens's larger ambition for *Martin Chuzzlewit* is evident, too, in its failures. In his eagerness to press his point, he belabors it, and the first chapters of the novel are tedious and wordy. This tendency to expand upon each idea until it is driven into the ground is a feature of *Martin Chuzzlewit* more than of earlier or later novels, evidence that Dickens doesn't trust his readers to understand the larger theme of which he is enamored, and it gives the novel a tiresome quality. Critics who are impatient with Dickens's abundance and see it simply as surfeit have ammunition in *Martin Chuzzlewit*.

In fact, Dickens is attempting a bildungsroman unlike anything he has done before—his theme is the moral education of young Martin, whose origins in the selfish bosom of the Chuzzlewit family compromise his innocence in a way that Oliver's, Nicholas's, and Nell's have not been. The question of the narrative is whether or not Martin will go the same way as Jonas, his cousin, who is so much cast in the family mold that "he had gradually come to look, with impatience, on his parent as a certain amount of personal estate, which had no right whatever to be going at large, but ought to be secured in that particular description of iron safe which is commonly called a coffin, and banked in the grave." Martin's tale has no inherent structure, unlike Nicholas's tale, which takes its structure from the popular melodrama, or Oliver's tale, which takes its structure from orphan narratives. Nor is Martin himself of particular interest as a character; he is overshadowed by the changelessly grotesque comic figures like Pecksniff and Mrs. Gamp, in whose variations upon the theme of selfishness and solipsism the author finds more of interest.

In volume form, *Martin Chuzzlewit,* which was dedicated to Angela Burdett-Coutts, did sell well enough. Dickens himself was enthusiastic about it, no doubt for the same reason that he was enthusiastic about *The Old Curiosity Shop*—it satisfactorily expressed his state of mind while he was writing it. He was, in fact, coming up with a unified social vision, something that marks the maturation of every serious novelist, since the novel is first and foremost about how individuals fit, or don't fit, into their social worlds. That this novelist, just thirty, hadn't quite refined his ideas, that he belabored some of them, that some of them were unsophisticated and harsh, should come as no surprise. Equally, that he fell back upon his natural gifts of language, invention, and character drawing to get himself through, while failing at story construction, something he always had to work hard at, comes as no surprise, either. That his social, as opposed to what might be called his "interpersonal," vision would be dark surely had its source in the inequities, suffering, and indifference he saw around him. While by Dickens's time the novel had not yet become the dominant European literary form, it had been around long enough to explore one broad theme—the discovery of the World—and to begin upon the second: the exploration of domestic life. Dickens's own favorite novels, Henry Fielding's *Tom Jones* (Dickens named his eighth child and sixth son Henry Fielding Dickens), Tobias Smollett's *The Adventures of Roderick Random,* and Cervantes's *Don Quixote,* which Dickens loved as a child, all followed their heroes on adventures of discovery. What the heroes discovered was not as important, historically, as the conviction that there was something to discover, that whatever it was would be interesting, illuminating, or enriching in some way. This mimics the European adventure of discovering and colonizing the New World. The adventure winds up bitterly, in the hands of Voltaire, when Candide returns, resolved henceforth to cultivate his own garden. The assumption of adventure literature is that domestic life is by nature already known, worth hardly a backward glance. In addition, the domesticated Cunegonde, originally Candide's romantic inspiration, ends up as a drudge and a disappointment, hardly worth depicting.

By Dickens's time, in many ways as a result of Sir Walter Scott's interest not only in the hero and his adventure, but also in the social and domestic circumstances of the hero's world, domestic life becomes as interesting as the adventure; in Dickens's work, domestic life becomes the goal of the journey, the prospective haven from the alienation and cruelty of homelessness. Dickens's heroes and heroines take many journeys, but only the travels of the Pickwick Club are embarked upon willingly. Most often, the protagonist is ejected from his original home and forced out upon a quest to make another. Dickens's social vision is formed by the recognition that in the world around him there are few bonds of social responsibility or generous humanity linking class to class or individual to individual, and that the government speaks and acts only for a small portion of the citizens, whereas the majority have no voice, no power, and no privileges. By contrast, small social groups, such as families, groups of friends, theater companies, and gangs of thieves, can mediate between the isolated individual and the vast social machine. But their mediation and companionableness can go either way, morally and spiritually, depending upon whether the members are motivated by love and kindness or by greed and selfishness. In all of Dickens's early novels, at least one group represented the possibility of sociable safety and contentment—the Pickwickians, Mr. Brownlow's household, Nicholas's family and friends. In *Martin Chuzzlewit,* the selfish, greedy groups are dominant; Martin must find his way against a strong tide.

Much of what Dickens was trying to get at in *Martin Chuzzlewit* was distilled in nearly perfect, supremely popular, and highly theatrical fashion in *A Christmas Carol,* which Dickens conceived of suddenly a few weeks after visiting the Field Lane School for Miss Coutts. He worked on it during October and November 1843, while the tenth and eleventh numbers of the longer novel were appearing; and in spite of his vow of the summer, *A Christmas Carol* was published by Chapman and Hall. He delivered the manuscript in early December, to be published for the Christmas trade. In an effort to avoid the sorts of contractual problems he had encountered with the low sales of his longer novel, he agreed with the publishers to publish on a commission basis—that is, he would design, edit, and produce the book (rather like book packaging today). Unfortunately, his desire to produce a beautiful artifact as well as a popular story meant that production costs were very high, and he realized, once again, only a small profit on what turned out to be a very large sale.

A Christmas Carol, like *Martin Chuzzlewit,* concerns itself with the social ramifications of selfishness, but the characters of young Martin and old Martin are combined in that of Ebenezer Scrooge, and his moral journey, which takes place in three acts in one night, has the force of revelation rather than the tedium of a lengthy trek by ox-drawn wagon. Some of the narrative had its origins in one of Dickens's own vivid dreams, and surely the idea of using dreams as a structural device had its origins there as well. The thirty-one-year-old Dickens was evidently in a state of considerable psychological turmoil. He was beset by money worries and family obligations at the same time that Catherine was pregnant with a fifth child. He had found his experience at the Field Lane School disturbing, and he must have recognized the vast insolubility of the larger task no matter what he and Miss Coutts were able to do with her funds. He was halfway through a serialization that no one considered a success, and he was in conflict with his father and mother as well as with his publishers. Just as every literary character is the author in some guise, just as Ralph Nickleby and Daniel Quilp were "Dickensian," so Ebenezer Scrooge was Charles Dickens, a man for whom money itself offered the prospect of safety, a man for whom isolation from the obligations of human relationship might be a form of peace.

The story is familiar from countless renditions, takeoffs, and parodies. In fact, pirates began to appropriate Dickens's characters and ideas immediately upon publication. But what makes *A Christmas Carol* work—what makes it so appealing a novella that William Makepeace Thackeray, Dickens's most self-conscious literary rival, called it "a national benefit"—is the lightness of Dickens's touch. Instead of hammering his

moral points home, as he does in *Martin Chuzzlewit,* he is
content (or more content) to let his images speak for themselves. For example, when Scrooge returns home after business, he sees Jacob Marley's face in his door knocker:
"Marley's face. It was not in impenetrable shadow, as the
other objects in the yard were, but had a dismal light about it,
like a bad lobster in a dark cellar." Subsequently, ascending
his staircase, Scrooge sees a hearse in front of him, but he
seeks no more light than that of his candle—"Up Scrooge
went, not caring a button for that: darkness is cheap and
Scrooge liked it." After a further series of mysterious noises,
which Scrooge declines to believe in, Marley himself appears,
and Dickens's description of him is economical but perfectly
apt: "Marley in his pig-tail, usual waistcoat, tights, and boots;
the tassels on the latter bristling, like his pig-tail, and his
coatskirts, and the hair on his head. The chain he drew was
clasped about his middle. It was long, and wound about him
like a tail; and it was made (for Scrooge observed it closely) of
cash-boxes, keys, padlocks, ledgers, deeds, and heavy purses
wrought in steel. His body was transparent: so that Scrooge,
observing him, and looking through his waistcoat, could see
the two buttons on his coat behind." Not only are these details both picturesque and thematically evocative, they are
conveyed without any overbearing tone of self-display. Melodrama (which Dickens loved) always carries a lack of conviction, because the gestures of the characters and the tone of the
author overstate rather than understate the emotions that are
being conveyed. Here, Dickens's descriptions underscore
Scrooge's resistance to the implications of the scene, enhanc-

ing our sense of Scrooge's coldness, but also his bravery. Additionally, it enables the reader to see what is happening more clearly than if Scrooge's feelings cluttered the picture. Every line performs more than one literary function, something that is a hallmark of Dickens's best writing. When he is trying too hard, every line performs less than one function, simply because he elaborates until he is sure the reader gets it. Immediately in the next paragraph, Dickens goes for a laugh—"Scrooge had often heard it said that Marley had no bowels, but he had never believed it until now." Scrooge's state of mind is believably mixed. He is observant, alert, frightened but incredulous, stubborn, ironic, and, most of all, interested. The scene is a masterpiece of narrative depiction, conveying simultaneously what is being seen, who is seeing it, and the narrator's attitude toward it, as only narrative can do.

Dickens took easily to the form of the novella, understanding intuitively that in focus and scope it is similar to a play but offers a novelist the opportunity to explore a single idea in depth and, in a way, at leisure. He seems to have had no trouble controlling his natural expansiveness, which the serial form of publication both tested and encouraged. The musical model for the composition (not only are songs evoked in the title of the work, but each part is called a "stave") gave him a sure sense of rhythm and symmetry. The style is free, but the freedom stays within the tight confines of the plot—the first bit, Scrooge in company, disdaining others, balances the last bit, Scrooge in company, welcoming others, while the three dreams, of course, fall into the utterly natural symmetry of past, present, and future—what Scrooge has forgotten, what he is missing, and what might happen if he persists in his misanthropic ways. The philosophy and psychology of *A Christmas Carol* are so familiar to us now that we forget that in Dickens's own day, his views competed with much less sophisticated notions of the origins and effects of states of mind. Indeed, this idea—that shifts in objective conditions, such as wealth, social relationships, and class disparities, begin within the individual and are then manifested outwardly in material changes—runs counter to notions of materialism and determinism that were beginning to take hold among such political thinkers as Bentham, Marx, and Engels, who were at work in the same period. Karl Marx, in fact, seems to have been quite a fan of Dickens. But Dickens's Christmas stories (*A Christmas Carol, The Chimes,* and *The Haunted Man* in particular) are increasingly specific and pointed about where necessary social change must come from. It is not enough to seize power or to change where in society power lies. With power must come an inner sense of connection to others that, in Dickens's life and work, comes from the model of Jesus Christ as benevolent Savior. The truth of *A Christmas Carol* that Dickens understood perfectly and bodied forth successfully is that life is transformed by an inner shift that is then acted upon, not by a change in circumstances.

The conditions that so appalled Dickens constituted the major political and philosophical challenge of his era. The novel, like any other artistic form, makes an inherent philosophical assertion—that the mental life of the individual is worth anatomizing and that the disruptions that exist among individuals and between individuals and groups are understandable and soluble through individual transformation and action. Dickens expanded and expanded his canvas because he intuited that the complexities of the social dilemmas he was interested in could not be convincingly portrayed in miniature. Other thinkers, not novelists, had other ideas about the significance of individuals and individualism, but Dickens's chosen form saddled him with a philosophical question he tried ardently to solve, both artistically and personally, for his entire life. The controversies that arise about Dickens's real political views, in my opinion, arise primarily from the fact that a novelist always, and increasingly, sees the trees rather than the forest, and is naturally unsympathetic to a collective solution, while always more or less in favor of a connective solution.

When the first six thousand copies of *A Christmas Carol* showed a very small profit, owing to the expenses of production, Dickens panicked. He wrote Forster, "Such a night as I have passed! I really believed that I should never get up again, until I had passed through all the horrors of a fever" (meaning a serious, delirious illness), and added, "I shall be ruined past all mortal hope of redemption." He became convinced that he needed to remove his household of wife, sister-in-law, and five children to continental Europe, where they could live more frugally and where Dickens could write more travel pieces. Ackroyd points out that Dickens was afraid of overexposure. He did not want to wear out his welcome with his audience and possibly thought that it was overexposure that accounted for the continuing poor sales of *Martin Chuzzlewit.*

Catherine's pregnancy with Francis, the fifth child of the family in seven years, seems to have marked a turning point in Dickens's attitude toward his wife. The agitation he betrayed in his money worries and his eagerness to go abroad met with great reluctance and depression on her part. He seems to have held against her both the inconvenience of the pregnancy and her inability to rally quickly after the birth. The stresses of their life together accentuated their temperamental differences. Where perhaps he had valued her placidity in the past, now he grew impatient with it and was willing to air his impatience to friends. Georgina Hogarth, too, was a continued contrast to Catherine—quicker, younger, perhaps able to share Dickens's mental life more readily than her sister. The balance among the three was shifting, and Dickens seems at this point to have begun to have brief infatuations with young women. The first of these was an eighteen-year-old girl he met while giving a speech in Liverpool, Christiana Weller, in whose album he wrote, "I love her dear name which has won me some fame / But Great Heaven how gladly I'd change it." Some weeks later, a friend of his, T. J. Thompson, informed Dickens that he wished to marry Christiana, and Dickens asked him to save the dress Dickens had first seen her in, just as he had saved one of Mary Hogarth's dresses after she died.

When the family departed for the Continent at the end of June 1844, it is safe to say that every aspect of Dickens's life was in turmoil, including, again, his relationship with his publishers. With the end of *Martin Chuzzlewit,* he left Chapman and Hall for Bradbury and Evans, still smarting over the idea that fifteen months before, it had been suggested that he repay part of his *Chuzzlewit* advance. Finance, family life, relations with his parents, the direction of his work, his emotional attachments, and, of course, his domiciliary arrangements, all were in flux. He was determined that these worries were to be resolved in Genoa, where the family settled in a large house in the suburbs overlooking the sea.

CHAPTER THREE

IN THE TWO YEARS between the end of *Martin Chuzzlewit* and the beginning of *Dombey and Son,* Dickens tried several things that failed to come to fruition, each in a different way, and that were expressive of his unsettled mind and his anxiety about how he was to live with his well-populated family. The first of these, of course, was the move to Genoa, first to the Villa Bagnerello and then, at the approach of winter, to the Palazzo Peschiere, which was easier to heat. Over the course of his Italian sojourn, he wrote *Pictures from Italy* (to be published in 1846), and in October, eager to repeat the success of *A Christmas Carol,* he began to write *The Chimes,* which has a more explicit satirical purpose than the earlier work but is similar in theme. Trotty Veck—an impoverished ticket porter who carries messages and does small jobs—is accosted by a magistrate, a Benthamite, and another idle gentleman, who discuss his meal and his life in utilitarian terms. Afterward, he has a dream or a vision of his future: himself dead, his daughter worked to death, and her fiancé a drunkard. Once again, Dickens expresses his opinion that mental images create worldly conditions. To embrace the utilitarian view, or the puritanical view, or the Tory view, that poor people have no reason to live, or are inherently prone to evil, or are a burden on the rich, is to create a more than self-fulfilling prophecy—not only do the individuals themselves live joy-less, wasted lives, they are sundered from one another by suspicion and solipsism. Only connection, forgiveness, and hope can prevent such an outcome. *The Chimes* has not been nearly as popular as *A Christmas Carol*, and it was very controversial in its day, but it sold well and made Dickens a quick £1,000. As usual, it was faithful to his state of mind at the time he wrote it, so he was extremely pleased with it and went back to London for the publication, traveling alone by laborious stages.

Upon his return to Genoa, Dickens took up mesmerism. An Englishwoman, Madame de la Rue, had several long-standing complaints that Freud might have called hysterical and we might call schizophrenic. Dickens successfully hypnotized her over and over; during these sessions, he elicited background material and gave her instructions. The progress of her condition was in some ways alarming, but Dickens's confidence in his "treatment" never flagged, and he persisted, ultimately affording her considerable lasting relief from the conviction that she was being visited at night by a phantom. For Dickens, of course, this "relationship" had irresistible fascination. For one thing, he became intimate to an unusual degree with just the sort of mental pathology and extreme idiosyncrasy that he always found interesting, and for another, his "treatment" was working, which he admitted gave him a sense of power. For a third, the relationship was with a woman, therefore it could be intimate and platonic at the same time. We can only marvel at how, once again, something that turned up in Dickens's life, like his American celebrity, uncannily presaged a common feature of our time—the therapeutic relationship. That Dickens should prefigure Freud makes wonderful sense, since Freud loved Dickens and since both Freud and Dickens were essentially highly observant storytellers who gave large meanings to very small details and actions, creating worlds of interlocking meaning out of, in particular, repetition, unconscious actions, and habitual interactions. But Dickens's pleasure and interest in his "treatment" of Madame de la Rue aroused a protest from Catherine, perhaps her first ever, and even though he was nettled by her reaction, he cooled the relationship. As with acting, perhaps, "therapy" was a great talent Dickens could have developed if circumstances had fallen differently.

While not exactly giving up his desire to live abroad, Dickens returned to England periodically and involved himself in yet another aborted scheme that redounded less well to his reputation, the founding of a daily newspaper. Dickens's new publishers, Bradbury and Evans, thought it a good time to start a newspaper to rival the *Times* and the *Morning Herald,* but with radical sympathies. Much of the money was railroad money, and the railroad was the transforming technological news of the day. Controversy surrounding *The Chimes* had proved both profitable and enlivening; how better to build upon it than to make the famous Charles Dickens editor of a paper that would institutionalize his liberal views? Dickens was equally enthusiastic and entered with fervor into the planning of the first editions. He hired the staff (including his father, John Dickens, as manager of the parliamentary reporters). There was a setback—one of the money men went bankrupt. Dickens resigned. But the investors reorganized and found more money, and the project went forward again.

In the meantime, Dickens wrote his third Christmas book, *A Cricket on the Hearth,* which had no social dimension at all but was the tale of a jealous elderly man and his young wife, perhaps, according to Ackroyd, a reworking of Dickens's own marriage with the genders reversed. There are two important things about *A Cricket on the Hearth.* One of them is that work on the newspaper affected the time and attention Dickens was able to devote to his narrative. The other is that it was a commercial success, selling twice as many copies as *The Chimes.* That the Christmas books established ever more clearly Dickens's direct relationship to his public was of great importance to him, and all the more important as the first issues of the *Daily News* began to take shape.

January 21, 1846, was the first day of publication, and it was not quite a success—there were typos and mistakes; Dickens was dissatisfied with his staff and his work arrangements. It quickly became clear that the project was not going to work as planned, and on February 9, Dickens resigned. In fact, his resignation was considered appropriate by most parties, since he was not exactly suited to the day-to-day detail work of an ambitious newspaper—there was too much of it, and he was constitutionally incapable of delegating editorial duties, as other experiences with weekly and monthly periodicals showed. Nevertheless, at first the transition seemed like a crisis—Dickens had formed the staff and the paper as much in his own image as possible, and there was some question about whether it could go on without him. But the crisis passed, and John Forster became the editor for about nine months. After that, the paper grew and established itself and continued to publish into the twentieth century. The contradictions in Dickens's character—his impulsiveness, his energy, his resistance to being the least bit fettered, and his readiness to blame others—all emerged in this battle, and the partners complained both that he was not doing his job well and that he didn't want to do it any longer. Clearly, however, editing a daily newspaper, while it appealed to the commercial, social, and political sides of Dickens's character, did not appeal to his deeper need to make art.

Dickens decided to relocate to the Continent again, and this time he chose Lausanne, Switzerland. He and Catherine now had still another son, Alfred, born at the end of October 1845, the sixth child and fourth son. Dickens was thirty-four. In ten years, he had written six full-length novels and three novellas, not to mention any number of occasional pieces. He had fathered six children. He was still working with Angela Burdett-Coutts on charitable projects, most notably the home for reformed prostitutes, Urania Cottage. He was directing, producing, and performing in ambitious amateur plays (in 1845, Dickens and some friends did a production of Ben Jonson's play *Every Man in His Humour*). His energy, sociability, and liveliness still struck everyone, including, now, his children, who recalled later how much fun he had been in their early childhoods, playing with them, chatting with them, charming them, attending to them with particular affectionate concentration that caused them to adore him in return.

Lausanne was clean, quiet, and pretty. Shortly after arriving there, at the end of June 1846, Dickens went back to his real work and began to write *Dombey and Son*. As with *Martin Chuzzlewit,* he had been planning the structure of *Dombey and Son* carefully and as a whole. He also, from the beginning, intended to introduce some autobiographical material and based the establishment of Paul's "caretaker," Mrs. Pipchin, on a woman he had stayed with as a boy. But *Dombey* is different from earlier novels in that the protagonist, the character to be transformed, is an already mature man who bears some resemblance to Scrooge rather than to the many youthful heroes of earlier works. This choice immediately gives the novel more structural coherence—Dombey is an established man with a household, a mode of life, a set of acquaintances, and a very particular agenda. It is his certainty and pride that form the world of the other characters.

Dombey and Son, like several other nineteenth-century works (*Vanity Fair,* for example, which was published at the same time, and *A Doll's House,* and "The Death of Ivan Ilyich") concerns the commodification of familial relationships. Dickens is explicit—of Dombey's estimation of his daughter Florence, he writes in the first chapter, "But what was a girl to Dombey and Son! In the capital of the House's name and dignity, such a child was merely a piece of base coin that couldn't be invested—a bad boy—nothing more." When Paul Dombey is born, as proud and pleased as his father is, the man gets no present enjoyment from his child but only anticipates their future business partnership. Impatient to get the necessary processes of childhood, like illnesses and education, out of the way, he hardly notices Paul's actual circumstances—delicacy and ill health—and is astounded to be informed of them. Nor does he experience the affection of his favorite child, who is cared for by others and who rather shrinks in his father's presence. He looks upon the love between Paul and Florence with jealous impotence. The sight moves him to envy, and to spite toward Florence, but not to any form of self-doubt or introspection. What is especially interesting about Dombey is that the origins of his pride and remoteness are not at all investigated. His identification as a wealthy merchant serves to explain why as well as what he is. It is this sense of Dombey's character originating in his business life that differentiates him from Scrooge, for example, and makes *Dombey and Son* all the more pointed a critique of capitalist relationships.

Dickens was pleased with the first numbers of *Dombey and Son* but found the going difficult. He attributed this to being away from London. He wrote Forster, "A day in London sets me up and starts me. But the toil and labor of writing, day after day, without that magic lantern, is IMMENSE!!" Nevertheless, theme, story, and, most important, style fell together seamlessly in the new novel. A great novel is, as much as anything else, an exercise of sustained stylistic felicity, and everyone—Dickens, Forster, other friends, the critics, and the public—recognized with the first number that Dickens had uncovered his sharpest, easiest, and most flexible voice. The first paragraphs draw us in effortlessly, wittily, and economically. The scene has a momentary stillness and intimacy, like a movie close-up. The father, sitting beside the fire, is connected to the newborn son, drawn up to the fire in his basket. Both are bald, red, and not quite beautiful; both are subject to the depredations of time. We are asked immediately to regard them not only as characters and agents of the story, but as objects of contemplation. The invitation is graceful, almost homely—the son is likened to a muffin; his just born appearance is "somewhat crushed and spotty in his general effect, as yet," but out of the simplest of contrasts between the baby and the man, Dickens draws a beautifully evocative figure: "The countenance of Son was crossed and recrossed with a thousand little creases, which the same deceitful Time would take delight in smoothing out and wearing away with the flat part of his scythe, as a preparation of the surface for his deeper operations."

Dickens's tonal and stylistic choices were always remarkable for their richness and variety. He could do low comedy, melodrama, farce, fairy tale, confession, sarcasm, lyricism, romance, extended analogy, dialect imitation. He had an ear for every sort of discourse, both written and oral. He did not always use an elevated literary style, something for which he was criticized in his time. He was not always considered to be in control of his material, but rather he was sometimes accused of being carried away, into sentimentality or tastelessness. Certainly, in *Martin Chuzzlewit,* extended use of personification and figurative language to little apparent purpose had tried his audience. But the control he shows throughout the nine hundred pages of *Dombey and Son* is exceptional, especially for a novelist publishing in serial parts. Certain critics have pointed out that the characters of the novel are particularly "Dickensian"—that is, they show vivid, repetitive, almost mechanically unchanging behaviors. Only the most extreme challenges can wrench them out of the habitual modes of expression and behavior. In part because the novel is a kind of tableau vivant, this "Dickensian" effect works better here than in some of the other novels, but because the characters are very distinct, the author has to vary the tone and style of the narrative. The style of *Dombey* routinely accomplishes all of this. Chapter 29, for example, where Dombey's sister informs Miss Tox of Dombey's engagement to Edith, is a hilarious set piece, where the mutually exclusive viewpoints of the two women, the brother-in-law, the spying Major Bagstock, and Major Bagstock's Eastern servant all clash and contrast, only to be briefly but gracefully resolved in the last paragraph, with the narrator's own voice: "While poor excommunicated Miss Tox, who, if she were a fawner and a toad-eater, was at least an honest and a constant one, and had ever borne a faithful friendship towards her impeacher, and had been truly absorbed and swallowed up in devotion to the magnificence of Mr. Dombey—while poor excommunicated Miss Tox watered her plants with her tears, and felt that it was winter in Princess's Place."

Dickens's characters in general have often been criticized for not being "realistic" or "rounded," especially his women characters. Certainly they contrast with those of, say, George Eliot or Henry James. Whether this contrast arises from something lacking in Dickens or something present in Dickens that is not present in the others (comic exaggeration, for example), Dickens's characters often seem weirdly truer to life than those of more realistic novelists. While some readers consider the oft-repeated calling cards of some characters evidence of one-dimensionality, in fact, it is a standard literary device to give minor comic characters taglines or bits of repeated business so that they can distinguish themselves. Additionally, such calling cards are features of romance as well as the literature of the spiritual journey, such as *Pilgrim's Progress,* in which a rather colorless hero meets personifications of tests, challenges, or qualities that he needs to assimilate in order to achieve his goal. Dickens, with his many innocent heroes and heroines from Pickwick to Esther Summerson, clearly writes in these traditions. Furthermore, the novel as a genre is particularly capacious in terms of the confluence of theme and form. That it is written in prose seems to make it more naturally "realistic," but in fact it may use the devices of any type of narrative. Dickens repeatedly pushed the English novel away from standard realism at the same time that he pushed it away from depicting the English bourgeoisie. He expanded the social/economic scope of the novel while expanding its linguistic resources with no regard for class status or stylistic propriety—he gave his narrator and his array of characters many tongues to speak in, quite a few of which were visionary or poetical, and which themselves undermined the "realism" of the form. Ultimately, he required, or allowed, the reader to regard more of the life around him by allowing it to be important enough to get into a novel. He thereby expanded the audience of the novel itself.

We may add to this by pointing out Dickens's pivotal position in the shift in English literature from a countryside-based production to an urban-based production. Not only does Dickens's work look back to *Pilgrim's Progress,* it looks forward to Dostoevsky, Freud, and Kafka, three authors who were greatly influenced by Dickens. Many of Dickens's characters seem diagnosable, at least as harmless neurotics, but sometimes as murderous psychotics or tormented obsessive-compulsives or manic-depressives. How they present themselves has the repetitive clarity of mental dysfunction translated into social dysfunction. In his comic mode, the characters manage to overcome the isolation attendant upon their individual dysfunctions and connect with one another. In his tragic mode, they do not, but instead suffer further isolation and death. The question is not whether Dickens's characters are "realistic," like those of Jane Austen, but whether he makes a compelling case for the origins and resolutions of their dilemmas, which are, in many cases, extreme and melodramatic. These are exactly the terms in which most people experience their own dilemmas—life-or-death propositions that are tremendously challenging to resolve. Kafka, for example, often wrote of his conflict with his father as if one or the other of them had to die. Freud depicted the suffering of "the Wolf-man" and of "Dora" (named after David Copperfield's first wife) in vivid terms, even though to the average reader their problems seem almost negligible. Dickens excelled at bodying forth the drama of the inner battle. Sometimes it is truly an inner battle, as in Scrooge or in Edith Dombey. Other times it seems to be a social or political battle, as in *Barnaby Rudge* or *Oliver Twist,* but the resolution always takes place within the character first and then in the social nexus. The difference between Dickens and Dostoevsky or Kafka has to do with the persistence of the social and political world. The very thing that Dickens worked against, and grew increasingly frustrated by in his social concerns—that is, the apparent resistance to change of English society—is what gives the world of his novels their reassuring comic stability. Conditions don't change, but people can; so Dickens, his characters, and his readers are afforded some measure of relief while still protected from the sort of terrifying vertigo that is a feature of later European literature.

Charles Dickens was a secretive man. Acquaintances, friends, relatives, and children always commented upon the fact that he could withdraw as readily as he could extend himself, that while he was so eagerly observing others he was also resisting observation himself. In our own time we see that great celebrity creates secretiveness, because the natural middle ground of private life is so difficult of attainment for those who live in the eye of the media. Certainly, secretiveness as an aspect of celebrity operated intermittently in Dickens's life—especially during his sojourn in America, where his fans were much more intrusive than his English ones. But the larger part of Dickens's secretiveness had deeper origins and longer-lasting effects. The fact is that modern readers know more of Dickens's early life than any of his contemporaries, including his wife and children, precisely because he made it his business to keep his family origins and his childhood to himself. There are several aspects to this. For one, Dickens did not come from a respectable family. His father, John Dickens, was persistently impecunious. Though he had many jobs and did well at them, he was not able to live within his income and had a habit of not only borrowing from his son, but also trying to make money by selling Dickens's manuscripts and autographs behind his back or approaching Charles's friends and asking for loans. Dickens's mother, Elizabeth Barrow Dickens, was the daughter of Charles Barrow, who worked as a clerk at the Navy Pay Office. In 1810, the year John and Elizabeth's first child, Fanny, was born, Charles Barrow was discovered to have embezzled several thousand pounds and escaped the country before he could be prosecuted. Most of Dickens's antecedents came from the serving class rather than the professional or propertied classes. The routine and even required American process of leaving one's origins behind was much more difficult in England, even in the England of Dickens's time, which was undergoing a vast social shift. Dickens's friends—Maclise, Macready, Wilkie Collins, and Forster himself—were usually men who, like Dickens, had used talent and energy to make their own way. But as they rose in economic and social status, they encountered more conservative elements of society, men and women who gave them respect for their accomplishments, but a respect always circumscribed by reservations about dress, or education, or behavior, or modes of speaking. Dickens's colorful manner of dressing, for example, was always judged as a bit déclassé. The sheer weight of his talent and charm gained him passage pretty much wherever he wanted to go in English society, but it did not gain him the invisibility of perfect acceptance. One index of this was the difficulty his daughters had, later on, in making good marriages. For all these reasons, Dickens's secretiveness and shame at his origins was a realistic response to the closed, judgmental nature of English social life.

But Dickens's shame was not merely social embarrassment, and in the months after the completion of *Dombey and Son* he seems to have understood intuitively that his growth as an artist depended upon the excavation of his boyhood and the revelation of some of those experiences. The success of *Dombey* permitted this in several ways. One was that the novel was a rousing success, both critically and financially, and the terms of Dickens's contract with Bradbury and Evans meant that he profited handsomely. He became financially secure and remained so thereafter (though he was at times beset by worries, especially late in life). Another was that he had approached one of the critical episodes of his childhood through the depiction of Mrs. Pipchin, and he had enjoyed writing about it. From the evidence of *Dombey,* he had, as it were, reduced her to her proper size—his adult mind had come to comprehend her and his power over his childish self, and he had experienced one of the special privileges of writing novels—putting powerful early experiences into a context. That Dickens felt a kinship with his former friend Madame de la Rue seems undeniable. That he helped her find a process for contextualizing and releasing herself from ideas and fears that oppressed her seems equally undeniable. Now he was ready to do something similar for himself, and he set about it with his usual energy. No doubt an additional motivation was the death from tuberculosis of his sister Fanny, only thirty-eight years old.

Dickens had finished writing *Dombey* at the end of March 1848. The final number appeared in April, when the novel was also published in volume form. In April, Dickens and several friends also put on eight performances of *The Merry Wives of Windsor* as well as another farce, for the charitable benefit of the purchase of Shakespeare's birthplace in Stratford. Catherine was pregnant again, with the Dickenses' eighth child, sixth son. (Sydney, son number five, was two.) As Frederick W. Dupee notes, "To his more and more open dismay, she continued to bear him children at brief intervals. . . ." The modern reader must wonder how he expected her to stop bearing these children, but nineteenth-century sources don't engage substantively with the harder dilemmas of reproductive rights and choices. Ackroyd notes only that while Dickens's friend Wilkie Collins was reputed to have recourse to the seamier side of London life, and while Dickens showed no judgment of, and some interest in, Collins's activities, there is no evidence that Dickens himself conducted his sexual life with anything but the greatest propriety. He was a firm believer in the Victorian domestic ideal of male-female familial companionship, except that the companion he had chosen was proving less and less satisfactory.

During this time, it is not clear exactly when, Dickens began to write an autobiography. The fragment, amounting to some seven thousand words, was written, according to Forster, without any corrections, evidence of strong feeling and much previous thought. Its subject was a period he had not otherwise talked about, which has since become the most famous of his early life—at twelve, young Charles was removed from school and sent to work at a shoe polish factory, where he stood in a little window, pasting labels onto bottles, where passersby could watch him. Warren's Blacking Factory was situated by the Thames in London, at Hungerford Stairs, near the Strand (next to Hungerford Market, which was torn down when Charing Cross Station was built upon the site). We now associate the area with tourism and shopping, but before the neighborhood was rebuilt and Trafalgar Square was created, it was ancient, damp. And frightening to young Charles, who later wrote, "My whole nature was so penetrated with the grief and humiliation of [the experience] that even now, famous and caressed and happy, I often forget in my dreams that I have a dear wife and children; even that I am a man; and wander desolately back to that time of my life." Not long after Charles went to work (living at the lodgings of Mrs. Roylance, who was the original of Mrs. Pipchin), John Dickens was taken into custody for nonpayment of debts, and the rest of the family moved into the Marshalsea Debtors' Prison, on the south side of the river, across London Bridge.

Every biographer of Dickens has noted the profound impact these events had upon the boy and the man and speculated about the reasons. Certainly the change was fairly sudden and amounted to a class humiliation for the boy. Dickens had been born in Portsmouth, where his father worked in the Navy Pay Office, a respectable and promising appointment. His sister Fanny was about fifteen months older; two years later, his brother Alfred was born but died as an infant, and, two years after that, his sister Letitia. The Dickenses were, in fact, a large family, and by all accounts Charles came legitimately by his sociability, energy, and lively spirits, since the parents enjoyed singing, dancing, celebrating, and performing and encouraged the children's talents. The family lived briefly in London, and then the Navy Pay Office sent John Dickens to Chatham, a naval town on the Thames estuary, when Charles was five. Three more children were born by the time Charles was ten, making seven in all.

The five years in Chatham constituted Charles Dickens's happy childhood. He was, by his own account, very attached to his sister Fanny, and Chatham was an interesting place to grow up in—a naval town still resonating from the Napoleonic Wars, where much of the population was attached to the military in some way. It was a rough town, but Dickens always spoke of it more fondly than he spoke of neighboring Rochester, a more respectable cathedral town that Dickens considered oppressive. He was taught to read by his mother and then sent off with his sister to a nearby school when he was about six. He reported over and over as an adult that the great resource and joy of his childhood had been books—eighteenth-century novels, like *Peregrine Pickle* and *Tom Jones,* but especially *Tales from the Arabian Nights.* Adults who knew him in childhood commented upon his devotion to reading, and it seems evident that his parents were eager to supply him with both education and books (his mother taught him some Latin). But John and Elizabeth Dickens's good intentions were overwhelmed by their improvidence, and the fiscal life of the family got shakier and shakier.

When John was sent to London in the summer of 1822, now the father of seven, he simply could not live on his pay, and even though he enrolled Fanny in the Royal Academy of Music, Charles's schooling apparently came to an end. He had thought he was going to be educated for some profession, and it appeared that those hopes were to be utterly given up. His sister Fanny was not, by contrast, required to leave her studies. Ackroyd suggests that the humiliation of doing his work in the window of the blacking factory and being observed by passing strangers was especially galling to a child of Dickens's sensitivity—the nightmare counterpart to performing songs and speeches, which he always enjoyed. He had a horror of the factory and the district, and portrayed them later on as representations of evil and corruption. He was ejected from his family—while they lived rather comfortably together in the debtors' prison, he was required to make his way through the streets alone, purchasing his own provisions and running the gauntlet of all the street people and eccentrics who might notice him. He was small and unprotected and suddenly required to grow up without sympathetic companionship. And yet, of course, as he well knew then and later pointed out to his readers over and over, there were thousands of children in London suffering under far greater danger and hardship. His servitude lasted five months, after which his father's debts were relieved by a providential act of Parliament. His mother (no doubt attracted by the idea of a little extra money and one less mouth to feed) was reluctant to end his employment—something that Dickens never forgot or forgave; but he did go back to school for a few more years, before leaving finally at fifteen and embarking on his working life.

Dickens had other memories of childhood, some of them cherished. It was not only the unpleasant ones that compelled him as he began to address his early life in his work. In her last weeks, his sister Fanny had recounted to him an odd experience, which he related to Forster: "In the night, the smell of the fallen leaves in the woods where we had habitually walked as very young children had come upon her with such strength of reality that she had moved her head to look for strewn leaves on the floor at her bedside." Dickens's characteristic hypersensitivity to everything, but especially to sensory experiences, surely was a permanent feature of his makeup, and, of course, he had an extraordinary and well-developed memory. The impressions left by his childhood were a treasure; in order to revisit them, he had to rob the darker ones of their power, which he began to do through the autobiographical fragment. The fragment portrays the young Charles as the hapless victim of those around him, which Dickens the experienced author certainly sensed was not quite right, rhetorically, for a work that was to see publication. Confession and self-regard are the trickiest forms of rhetoric, the most likely to arouse ridicule or antagonism in the reader. Dickens the editor could distinguish between a document that had value for the author in organizing memories of experience and a document that had value for the reader in telling an entertaining or enlightening story. The autobiographical fragment didn't succeed, and Dickens subsequently sent it to Forster, who waited until after Dickens's death to publish it.

In the autumn, Dickens wrote his last Christmas book, *The Haunted Man.* The haunted man in question, a chemist named Redlaw, is an isolated scholar beset by memories of the death of his sister and of his betrayal by a trusted friend, who many years before had seduced away Redlaw's beloved. Like Scrooge, he is visited by a ghost, who offers to remove his faculty of memory and to give him the power to do likewise for everyone he meets. A kind and benevolent man, Redlaw suffers so much with his memories that he accepts this gift. In *The Haunted Man,* Dickens makes his most explicit argument for the primacy of mental attitude over external circumstances in the achievement of peace, happiness, and even prosperity. Redlaw's associates and acquaintances live in more problematic circumstances than he does—Mrs. Williams, his housekeeper at the college, has never had children after the death of her firstborn. Her eighty-four-year-old father-in-law has seen his older son lead a life of increasing depravity. One of Redlaw's students is recovering from a life-threatening illness and is impoverished. Neighbors of this student, the Tetterbys, have little money, little space, and too many children. But until Redlaw comes along, everyone is happy enough. In particular, the portrait of the Tetterbys is one of Dickens's very best evocations of family life and absolutely sparkles with a sense of lived experience. There is even a touch of homely forgiveness, since Mr. Tetterby is a small man and Mrs. Tetterby is fat (something Dickens seems to have held against Catherine). But every time Redlaw interacts with another character, even incidentally, that character loses his or her memories and is transformed. The effect is illustrated comically with the Tetterbys: "The hand of every little Tetterby was against the other little Tetterbys; and even Johnny's hand—the patient, enduring, and devoted Johnny—rose against the baby! Yes. Mrs. Tetterby, going to the door by mere accident, saw him viciously pick out a weak place in the suit of armour where a slap would tell, and slap that blessed child." The other characters are transformed as well, until Redlaw comes to realize the horrifying manner in which he is remaking the world and seeks reversal of his gift. Dickens's explicit point is that memories of both pleasure and suffering are the source of forgiveness and, indeed, the source of our capacity to live with one another in toleration and happiness. Without memories, only the present inconveniences of life can assert themselves, breaking connections and driving people apart.

Whether or not this philosophical assertion is true, Dickens worked it out in detail in *The Haunted Man* and then built upon it when he began perhaps his greatest, and certainly his favorite, novel, *David Copperfield,* in February 1849. It was just around the time of his thirty-seventh birthday, and exactly twenty-five years after the commencement of his employment at Warren's Blacking Factory.

It was Forster who suggested that Dickens use the first-person point of view to tell the story. He was possibly influenced by the popularity of *Jane Eyre,* published in 1847, though Dickens himself never read it. Dickens was no longer alone in the field of the Victorian novel—the publication of *Vanity Fair* coincided with that of *Dombey and Son.* Thackeray's feelings of rivalry (which Dickens does not appear to have shared) could not have been soothed by the comparative sales of the two novels—five thousand for each number of *Vanity Fair,* thirty thousand for *Dombey. Wuthering Heights* was published in 1847 as well, and Mrs. Gaskell's *Mary Barton* in 1848. Dickens was still the most popular serious novelist of the age, but other voices were emerging from his shadow, expressing distinct visions of their own. That they fed his inspiration, at least secondhand, is another manifestation of Dickens's natural inclusiveness. He seems to have been far less aware of them as rivals than they were of him— throughout his writing life, he was the primus inter pares. Writers who lived during his lifetime (and just after) felt they had to define themselves in relationship to him, but he did not reciprocate the feeling—he was generous with praise and invitations to write for the periodicals he edited, and honest, though tactful, with criticism. His own work filled up his thoughts while he was creating it; he paid no attention to what other writers might be doing.

David Copperfield did not go as smoothly or easily at first as *Dombey*. His letters to Forster were filled with complaints, and certain details, such as the title of the novel, the names of some characters, and the nature of David's profession, remained undecided or were changed well into the composition of first numbers, evidence of indecisiveness that was unusual for Dickens and in contrast with the high degree of planning that had worked so well for *Dombey*. Nevertheless, and even though *David Copperfield* sold fewer copies than *Dombey*, Dickens grew increasingly pleased with it and wrote steadily, without interruption.

He loved it as if it were his autobiography, but in fact the incidents of the novel and the incidents of Dickens's early life were quite different. David Copperfield, of course, is the scion of a much different family from the populous and convivial Dickenses. His father, twenty years older than his mother, is already dead by the time David is born. He lives happily with his mother and the servant, Peggotty, near Yarmouth. His father's sister, Betsey Trotwood, is a woman of property, though eccentric and embittered by her failed marriage. The first chapters of *David Copperfield* detail a sort of early childhood idyll, with David the treasured male child, that is brutally ended by David's mother's remarriage to Mr. Murdstone. Murdstone and his sister, Jane, are classic portraits of just the sort of Victorian parents that Dickens detested. They are harsh, serious, authoritarian, and unimaginative. Their cruelty arises from their own joylessness and lovelessness. Their most evil effect comes not from how they treat David and his mother (which is bad enough), but from how they cast a pall of heavy sobriety and restraint over everything. What Murdstone says is just close enough to what a typical stepfather might say to or about his stepson as to be especially chilling. When David bites Murdstone in the midst of being punished, he is sent away to boarding school.

The characters of Peggotty and her brother, Ham, Little Em'ly, and Barkis the carrier have no known analogues in Dickens's family, nor had Dickens ever been to Yarmouth until just before he began the novel. Nevertheless, *David Copperfield* seemed to Dickens to evoke the feelings he had had as a child, and therefore to be true to his life as he had experienced it. The events themselves were less important than the feelings they gave rise to in the author, and the first-person point of view allowed Dickens to evoke how it feels to be a child. This was certainly one of his special talents, and in *David Copperfield,* he did better than he had in *Oliver Twist* and *The Old Curiosity Shop* in mediating between a growing child's sense of his own power and his sense of being in the power of others. David is not a hapless victim; in fact, once he gets to school, his immaturity and ignorance hurt others, most notably Mr. Mell, whose family circumstances David knows he should not reveal but does anyway, leading to Steerforth's ridiculing Mr. Mell and Creakle's firing him. While we never lose sympathy for David, we also never forget that he has a task, which is to learn how to be a good man—his innocence is no guarantee of good judgment or right action. In this sense, the portrayal of David is far more sophisticated than earlier portrayals of children; even Paul Dombey is characterized at one point as sometimes imperious but never shown to be other than unusually wise and loving. The depiction of David's infancy and childhood is the sine qua non of such later depictions of childhood as the first chapters of

Portrait of the Artist as a Young Man. Dickens's experience and his natural sympathies with children in general led him to understand that the tone and style of childhood are different from that of adulthood and worthy of artistic representation. This is surely in part the reason Freud was so fond of *David Copperfield*—Dickens apprehended that the symbolic world of the small child was rich and had lifelong power, and in the course of relatively few pages of text, the life is lived and the symbolic links are forged. The narrative also reinforces the idea that a consciousness can understand how it came to be through memory and reconstruction of early experiences. David has no "analyst," but the narrator himself serves as the analyst, mediating through language and selection of incident between the reader and the protagonist.

The death of David's mother ends his schooling at Creakle's institution. He returns to Blunderstone for the funeral and subsequently is sent to work at the counting house of Murdstone and Grinby, wine merchants. He lodges with the Micawbers, but soon Mr. Micawber is arrested for debt and the Micawbers move into the King's Bench Prison. Of his working life, David notes, "All this time I was working at Murdstone and Grinby's in the same common way, and with the same common companions, and with the same ceaseless sense of unmerited degradation as at first. But I never, happily for me no doubt, made a single acquaintance, or spoke to any of the many boys whom I saw daily in going to the warehouse, in coming from it, and in prowling about the streets at meal-times. I led the same secretly unhappy life; but I led it in the same lonely, self-reliant manner." The contrast to Dickens's own life is specific. The Micawbers are comic representations of his parents; the counting house, while tedious and unpleasant, is not quite as appalling as the blacking factory. In fact, when Murdstone speaks to David before sending him out to work, he says something Dickens himself might have said: "To the young this is a world for action, and not for moping and droning in." The point is that David feels uncared for. It is not that he must make his way, but that no one cares whether and how he makes his way. Even the Micawbers are so wrapped up in their own affairs that David's ups and downs are of little moment to them. Certainly this is a true reflection of how Dickens experienced his parents when they were having difficulties—however pleasant and agreeable they were upon occasion, they were capable of no real understanding of or sympathy with him; it was as if he were simply their lodger.

David Copperfield evokes Dickens's life without relating it. The fiction frees him to contemplate not only his boyhood and young manhood, but boyhood and young manhood in general. David's task is simultaneously a moral one and an emotional one—to find true companionship but also to assume responsibility for one's choices and their consequences. Through observing those around him and also weighing his own actions and choices, David attains responsible manhood: at the end of the novel, he has a respectable career, good friends, and a soul mate in Agnes, who is often criticized for being dull and one-dimensional but is an interesting evocation of a quiet, self-contained, and responsible feminine presence. David succeeds fully where Dickens himself succeeded only partially—he was beginning to confide in Forster that he despaired of ever finding true intimate companionship.

The tenor of *David Copperfield* is comic, but because its

great subject is David's moral education, the happy ending does not quite balance out the costs of getting there. David and Agnes find each other, David's other loved ones live in prosperity and amity, Em'ly, Martha, and the Micawbers leave the scenes of their defeats to find new opportunities elsewhere. But Steerforth is lost, the Peggottys' lives are destroyed, and even Heep's defeat has a sour taste about it. The natural tendency of individuals to live in isolation through selfishness, greed, addiction, despair, and self-delusion is not *generally* mitigated—it is mitigated only in David's case, at least partly because he is lucky enough to find Agnes. There is no suggestion that he deserves Agnes, except insofar as he has learned enough to value her.

Both *Dombey and Son* and *David Copperfield* are great novels, but they succeed in part because they have backed away from larger social issues and allowed their protagonists to resolve problems that are representative of large social forces and dilemmas only as individuals. For a novel, such an individual solution is the only believable one, the only "realistic" one. At the same time, though, Dombey and David come to seem Cinderella-like—the form of the comic novel itself chooses them to prevail while all around them others succumb. The solution that Dickens bodies forth in each of his Christmas books, that of a change in a character's inner life creating outward change, works better as a parable than it does as a novel, because a novel needs more action to carry it than a single miraculous inner shift. As characters in a novel act upon one another and make their way in the world, the vivid sense of a single inner life is overwhelmed by the varied and multifarious strands of the narrative. Novels are both too short and too long. They are too short to reproduce, in rigorous depth, the moral development of more than a handful of characters, and too long to meditate upon philosophical issues without plenty of action to give those issues some narrative liveliness. Nevertheless, Dickens persisted in attempting to broaden and deepen the social meaning of his work, and of the novel itself, as subsequent works show.

David Copperfield ran from May 1849 to November 1850. Dickens was famously affected by its completion. He wrote in the preface, "An author feels as if he were dismissing some portion of himself into the shadowy world, when a crowd of the creatures of his brain are going from him forever." Reviews were at first mixed, and sales of the numbers not as good as those of *Dombey and Son*, but sales in volume form were good, and readers came around more and more to Dickens's own love for the novel. It has since become the quintessential Dickens novel, the easiest, the most appealing, the most frequently known for itself rather than through stage productions or movies. Between them, we may say, *Dombey and Son* and *David Copperfield* relieved Dickens of two of his profoundest anxieties—financial worries and residual fears from his youth. Both reconfirmed his continuing importance among contemporary novelists. In the next phase of his career, his relationships to everyone around him would shift as he built upon what *Dombey* and *Copperfield* had taught him.

CHAPTER FOUR

THE PERIOD while Dickens was writing *David Copperfield* was exceptionally productive even for him. At the end of 1849 he began to develop a new weekly periodical that came to be known as *Household Words,* "conducted by Charles Dickens." The first issue appeared on March 30, 1850. From this time forward, for some twenty years, he edited, wrote for, and profited from either this weekly magazine or his next one, *All the Year Round.* His editorship was active and informed, as well as lucrative, since he owned half of the magazine (which had a circulation of about thirty-five thousand), was paid £500 a year for editing it, and was also paid for contributions. He estimated that in 1850 alone he read nine hundred manuscripts, of which he accepted only a handful. His target audience with the magazine was the reading middle class that formed his earliest core audience, not intellectuals or artists or reformers, but a general readership that liked to be entertained and informed. He gathered around him a group of writers, who contributed anonymously. The only ones we know today were Wilkie Collins, author of *The Woman in White* and *The Moonstone,* and Elizabeth Gaskell, author of *North and South* and *Mary Barton.* Though not all of them liked the anonymity, one thing about working for Dickens appealed to all of them—he paid generously and quickly. He was also generous with editorial advice and even rewriting, which suited some authors more than others. But he had a particular vision—of informative articles and essays made more lively by his favorite mental activity, "fancy," and he was resolute in his assertion of his vision. As with the plays he directed and stage-managed, he felt responsible for every aspect of the production, but he also brought imagination, insight, and charm to working with the other egos involved. The many extant letters that he wrote to his authors attest to these qualities. As with his earlier forays into journalism, he was still attracted to "theme" issues—he would propose a theme, such as Christmas, and then he would write the opening and closing pieces while others would contribute variations on the theme (this had been the original idea behind *Master Humphrey's Clock*). In general, he worked to balance each issue, so essays taken out of context now can seem rather odd in tone, but as always, Dickens's primary artistic goal was to produce a first-rate whole. In the case of *Household Words*, which came out every Wednesday, the parts were secondary. At first Dickens worked with the assistance of John Forster. For most of his career, Dickens consulted Forster about all aspects of his work, from artistic choices to business concerns, and all of the novels show the effects of Forster's taste, which Dickens relied upon but in some cases overruled. Forster, who had an eighth share, and Dickens worked on *Household Words* together, apparently amicably at first, although they were beginning to disagree, because Forster's life and politics were growing more conservative.

With *Household Words,* Dickens became, if possible, more central to English literary life, because he accepted and published work by younger writers, who, according to most authorities, cherished even his rejection letters, they were so kind and full of support. He knew, and they knew, too, that he was "the Master." But he was by no means universally adored. Elizabeth Gaskell complained that *Household Words* was always "Dickensy." Even so, there were plenty of periodicals now, and novels, too, that were not by Dickens, or "Dickensy." We may say that he had built the mansion, but the mansion had come to have many rooms.

On August 16, Dickens's third daughter and ninth child was born. Dickens was just at that point in *David Copperfield* where he had to decide the fate of David's wife, Dora, and at around the same time that he decided she must die, he named his new baby Dora, which has caused some comment among biographers and, indeed, caused comment at the time. On the very afternoon of the birth, Dickens and the other children and Georgina Hogarth traveled from London to the family's usual summer resort, at Broadstairs. Catherine and the baby stayed home.

The third great enterprise in Dickens's life in the early 1850s was amateur play production. Dickens's interest in acting was always dedicated and enthusiastic, and between 1833 and 1847, he acted in a dozen plays. As *David Copperfield* was winding up, Dickens joined with Edward Bulwer-Lytton (author of *The Last Days of Pompeii* and many other works) to put on Ben Jonson's play *Every Man in His Humour,* and then one of Bulwer-Lytton's own, a comedy called *Not So Bad As We Seem*. These collaborations led to the formation of the Guild of Literature and Art, an insurance and retirement fund for authors and artists, "to render such assistance to both as shall never compromise their independence." As always, Dickens was eager to do good by having fun, and the two plays, plus a number of farces (including one where Dickens played six different characters), were performed off and on between May 1851 and September 1852.

Neither did Dickens stint his charitable work. He was still working with Angela Burdett-Coutts, helping her administer Urania Cottage. As with *Household Words,* he was a hands-on manager, directing everything, from 1847 until 1858, from staffing and organization to the management of daily crises. He continued to write about education and to promote schools for very poor children, and he took a strong interest in labor unrest and issues of sanitation and public hygiene. In other words, as his art was maturing and flowering, and as his financial footing was growing more and more secure, his other interests were finding greater, not lesser, expression. He was thirty-eight in 1850, and to all appearances, his stores of energy were vaster than ever, each enterprise stimulating the others, each calling forth just the right mix of principle, vision, dedication, hard work, and charm. Surely his treatment of his childhood, in *David Copperfield,* released him from old fears and enabled him to integrate all of his interests in an astonishing way. Commentators on Dickens's activities often say the same thing—what he did in each endeavor would have been uncommon enough in an average citizen, but in the greatest literary artist of his day, such energy and administrative genius were unprecedented.

In these years, though, his personal life afforded him several shocks, beginning with the death, already mentioned, of his sister Fanny, in August 1848. In March 1851, Catherine

Dickens's long-standing complaints came to a crisis. Ackroyd quotes a letter she wrote to a friend detailing her symptoms: "I have been suffering for some time from a fullness in the head, which has lately increased so much, & caused me such violent headaches &c, that I have been ordered to go at once to Malvern and try what change of air and cold water will do for me." Nine pregnancies in fifteen years had wrought a considerable change in Catherine Dickens. She had grown quite stout, for one thing, and was also subject to postpartum depression and anxiety. While acquaintances of the couple were often impressed by Catherine's cordiality and even temper, comparing them favorably with Charles's more unpredictable charms, Charles Dickens had been growing openly vocal about his dissatisfactions with his wife. The old balance between Catherine and Georgina, where each provided different sorts of companionship, had tipped in favor of Georgina, whom Dickens considered a close friend. He was kind and affectionate toward Catherine, but impatient with her clumsiness (which he had mocked in letters to Forster from America), her jealousy (which had upset him in Genoa, with the de la Rues), her general slowness, and her difficulties with pregnancy and childbirth. We may see that like many married couples, they had found their respective poles—his energetic, busy, irritable; hers placid, enervated, patient. Dickens had many bouts of ill health, but his response was to, if at all possible, work or run or walk it off. Hers was to succumb. Her characteristic modes of dealing with stress were increasingly irritating to him, proving not that she had her virtues, but that her virtues, in contrast with his, were not really virtues. Their incompatibility as a couple was evident to everyone, and would certainly have been evident to her, undoubtedly exacerbating her feelings of stress and his of dissatisfaction. Catherine went to Malvern, a spa, where the course of treatment would have involved cold baths, rest, fresh air, dietary changes, and possibly some exercise.

Then, on March 31, John Dickens, Charles's father, died. Dickens's relationship with his father had not been an easy one from the day John and Elizabeth took their oldest boy out of school and sent him to work in the blacking factory. Dickens had unsuccessfully attempted to distance himself from his father's improvident ways and had unsuccessfully attempted to employ his father in several of his editorial enterprises. He had spoken irritably of both his parents (and of his brothers, whose careers were more similar to John's than to Charles's), and Charles junior later reported that part of the reason the autobiographical fragment never made it into print was that Catherine had read it and considered the portrait of Dickens's parents too harsh. But once again, the writing of *David Copperfield* had reconciled many of these issues in Dickens's mind, and for the last years before his father's death, Dickens had come to treat him and speak of him with more affection and forgiveness. John Dickens's final illness came on rather suddenly. He was afflicted with bladder stones, and it was decided that an urgent operation to remove them was needed. When Dickens arrived after the operation (performed without anesthetic, of course) he said that his father's room looked like "a slaughterhouse." Though the elder man (John was sixty-six) was optimistic, the operation proved unsuccessful and he died six days later. Dickens was saddened and grieved by the death, and was also somewhat reconciled to his mother.

Shortly thereafter, on April 14, Dickens returned from a visit to Malvern to London to give a speech. At the end of the speech, Forster came up to him and told him that his infant daughter, Dora, only eight months old, had been suddenly taken ill with convulsions and had died that afternoon. The next morning, he wrote a note to Catherine, which Forster delivered, and he also postponed the evening's performance of the Bulwer-Lytton play. Two days later, one of his daughters reported, he broke down completely under the weight of his grief, but it was clear to everyone, including him, that when there were arrangements to be made, he was the one who had to make them. The performances resumed, *Household Words* continued on schedule, Catherine and the other eight children were cared for. As always, the remedy for grief was activity, with restless walks through the streets of London the substitute for sleep.

Also overcome by grief, Catherine returned from Malvern. In May, Dickens bought a new house, a large mansion called Tavistock House, and commenced renovations. He and the family went to their usual summer residence in Kent. In October, he began to write *Bleak House,* and its first number was published around the same time that the family moved into Tavistock House.

Although this is generally considered to be a dark time in Dickens's life, it is important to remember that Dickens was always capable of, and even eager for, fun. Ackroyd tells of the Twelfth Night party to which Dickens invited Thackeray and his daughters. As usual, there was a performance (Dickens had the new house fitted out with a small theater), which Dickens directed. At one point, five-year-old Henry came out and recited:

Now comes the conflabbergastation of the lovier
As Vilikins was valiking the garden around
He spied his dear Dinah laying dead upon the ground
And a cup of cold pison it lay by her side,
With a biller-dux a-stating 'twas by pison she died
Too ral lal, loo ral lal, too ral la.

"Thackeray," notes Ackroyd, "actually fell off his seat laughing."

In *Bleak House,* Dickens successfully integrated his social concerns with his narrative drive, rather than emphasizing the story, as he had done in *David Copperfield.* In so doing, he created a new sort of English novel, one that explores and questions the construction of English culture and society as a whole rather than merely certain institutions. Dickens locates the dilemmas and tragedies of his characters in institutions outside of their control and then analyzes how some characters fail while others manage to cope. In this, he departs somewhat from his earlier vision, in which the transformation of character and attitude allows for the transformation of the world. In *Bleak House,* the world is an impersonal and implacable machinelike place where all persons and things are in a state of constant devolution that can be halted or reversed only through the continuous exertion of taking responsibility and methodical hard work. There is no main character whose personal transformation or education is the central organizing principle of the work. Esther Summerson, who carries about half of the narrative, is defined at the beginning as self-effacing, orderly, and virtuous. Her real job is to serve as a witness to the moral educations of others, especially, but not only, of Richard Carstone and Caddy Jellyby.

The overarching metaphor of the novel is the ancient and costly Chancery suit of *Jarndyce* v. *Jarndyce,* and the location of much of the action is the area of London around the Inns of Court. In the very first chapter of the novel, Dickens ramifies the influence of the court of Chancery throughout England:

> . . . the court of Chancery . . . has its decaying houses and its blighted lands in every shire . . . its worn-out lunatic in every madhouse, and its dead in every churchyard; its ruined suitor, with his slipshod heels and threadbare dress, borrowing and begging through the round of every man's acquaintance.

Thereafter, the novel demonstrates the truth of this assertion—every character, no matter how highborn or lowborn, is connected to the suit of *Jarndyce* v. *Jarndyce*. In some instances, the connections seem gratuitous but turn out to be essential. The suit of *Jarndyce* v. *Jarndyce* is in fact an enormous family in which, try as any individual might, he or she cannot but experience his or her entangling relationship to the others. Against the background of the suit, individuals work out their fates by accepting their responsibilities, and their responsibilities are prescribed according to a familial model. *Jarndyce* v. *Jarndyce* is like an ecosystem where some degree of scarcity prevails. Only by husbanding the limited resources can everyone work out his or her fate to advantage, but the natural entropy of the system always threatens to overwhelm individual energies. And no single character's fate is of much greater interest than any other's. The novel is written on a large pattern; the pattern works itself out. The reality of connection is foregrounded, rather than the significance of individuals. The court of Chancery was not the boldest institution Dickens might have satirized—reviewers at the time pointed out that criticism was common and reform of the system was already taking place—but artistically, the fact that Dickens began with the institution rather than with individuals allowed him to create a larger world and to coordinate its parts more successfully than he had ever done.

Reviewers noted the impersonality of the novel. Forster didn't like it much, and Esther didn't go over well with anyone. Critics since then have argued whether Esther is a failure or not, and certainly her voice can seem coy and insincere, especially when she is reporting, only to discount, praises of herself. In subsequent years, Georgina Hogarth was willing to admit that Esther's character was based on hers (by contrast, she did not believe that Agnes Wickfield was based on her), and it must be the case that if Dickens was attempting to use someone he loved and honored as a model, he felt less free to depict her ironically, as he always felt free in depicting himself. The third-person narrative of *Bleak House* is exceptionally ironic in tone, even by Dickens's standard, and so the contrast makes Esther's narrative seem even stranger. And if Esther is Georgina, then John Jarndyce's relationship to her makes him a representation of Dickens himself—the guardian who pays for everything and takes care of everyone, yet who needs Esther as an intermediary between himself and the objects of his benevolence.

The second overarching metaphor that works with the first to bolster connection is the metaphor of disease. The theme of public sanitation had been important to Dickens at least since he was writing *Oliver Twist,* when he frequented the impoverished neighborhoods of Saffron Hill that stood right beside the house in Doughty Street where he lived with his family while writing the novel. Coincidentally, as he was writing *Bleak House,* he was also having workmen refurbish Tavistock House, including the plumbing and the drains; so waste management was on his mind. The problems mentioned in chapter 2, of a large population in a limited urban area, had not been solved by Parliament or the City of London, and would not be almost until Dickens's death. The figure of Jo embodied his old images of Ignorance and Want, always moving on, as Jo says of himself, but leaving behind a wake of death and destruction.

Bleak House is the most unhopeful of Dickens's novels. Characters such as Esther and Jarndyce at best succeed in holding off decay rather than transcending it or creating something from it. Every character is bound by his or her past, and the past cannot be escaped (as, for example, the Micawbers and Little Em'ly go off to Australia seeking a new life). Esther finds love and purpose in family life, but Allan Woodcourt is such a shadowy figure that their marriage is of no intrinsic interest. The comic side of Dickens's sensibility, the part of him that intuitively envisions integration and social redemption through laughter, is largely missing—here are no figures like Miss Tox and Mr. Chick, in *Dombey and Son,* or Barkis, Traddles, or Mr. Dick, in *Copperfield,* who are simultaneously ridiculous and benevolent and serve to connect the main characters in incidental but important ways. Harold Skimpole is a good example of a character whose foibles might have been treated more forgivingly in an earlier novel, but who comes to appear almost vicious by the end of *Bleak House.*

The stylistic felicity that marked *Dombey* and *David Copperfield* from beginning to end is more problematic in *Bleak House,* in large part because of Esther's narrative. David could easily narrate with Dickens's vision and, of course, was intended to do so—Dickens found a comfortable authorial distance from which he could both enter into David's mind and observe his growth—but Dickens cannot find a comfortable distance from Esther. Her voice is inconsistent—sometimes sharp-witted and sardonic, other times vapid. Finally, confining himself to her consciousness is difficult for the author. On the other hand, the third-person narrative suffers from too much irony—the famous first paragraph, about London fog, is telling but not subtle. Similarly to *Martin Chuzzlewit,* though to a lesser degree, Dickens has a point to make and wants to be sure the reader understands it clearly. During the 1850s, Dickens wrote to a correspondent that he did not write merely to entertain, but always with an improving object in mind, and this is evident in all of the works of that decade. Modern critics have rehabilitated *Bleak House,* admired its architecture and seriousness, as well as Dickens's attempts to negotiate a new kind of novel. Some critics have even forgiven the experiment of Esther's narrative on the grounds that she helps keep the extremely diverse story line under control.

One interesting feature of *Bleak House* is the character of Jo as analogous to the character of Topsy in Harriet Beecher Stowe's *Uncle Tom's Cabin,* which Dickens is known to have read while he was writing *Bleak House*. Jo, like Topsy, is an unreared child, Jo the mysterious product of unknown parents, Topsy the product of a slave-breeding operation. Both know nothing of their origins or of any conventional bits of knowledge, including religion. What is notable is that both authors, one writing the most popular novel in England and the other writing the most popular novel in America, were highlighting the "domestic" issue of how children develop a conscience and a sense of themselves through connection to others. Both show models of the relationship between well-regulated domestic life and well-regulated public life, a key part of that model being orderly relationships between responsible men and women living in the same households. The contrast between the fate of Topsy and the fate of Jo is especially illuminating—whereas Jo connects only to destroy, by carrying disease into the Jarndyce household, and then himself dies, a warning to the complacent classes, Topsy is reclaimed through systematic training and love. To Dickens, what Jo means is his main role in the novel; to Stowe, how Topsy gains a moral life is the important question.

Dickens was very happy with the sales of *Bleak House*. It sold about thirty-four thousand copies every number, beginning with the first number, and he profited by some £11,000. Sales were higher than *David Copperfield* by about fourteen thousand copies, and though reviews were mixed, public reception was enthusiastic. Dickens was now a rich man, as the purchase of Tavistock House demonstrated, and his contracts were always favorable to his interests. When his agreement with Bradbury and Evans came to be renewed at the end of *Bleak House*, it was renewed without fuss. Nevertheless, completing the novel was extremely taxing, and not only because it was a huge, complicated project. Ackroyd details the speeches, dinners, editorial work, outings, travels, house refurbishings, domestic duties (Dickens discovered that one of his sons had a stutter and commenced to train him out of it with a session in his study every morning), and correspondence that interfered with the production of the monthly numbers, and it is no surprise that at the completion of the novel, Dickens decided not to start another for at least a year.

In February 1852, Dickens turned forty years old. A month later, his tenth child and seventh son, Edward, was born. In one decade, the hopeful young man who had set sail for America had been transformed, in some sense, beyond recognition. His work was complex, dark, mature. Acquaintances no longer commented upon his boyishness. While he was still energetic and restless, and still capable of laughing frequently and uproariously, the duties he had taken on in his family, in his editorial capacity, in his role as social critic, and in his charitable work had made him a serious and even intimidating presence in English life. Reviewers who took issue with various aspects of *Bleak House* did so in the context of Dickens's mastery. His work was a known quantity; experimentation only reconfirmed that he always had something to say, always said it vastly and with vivid, melodramatic effects, with wit, invention, and "true and original genius" (as George Brimley noted in the *Spectator*). In spite of critics (even his friends Carlyle and Forster, for whom Dickens showed a great deal of respect, had reservations and suggestions) and in spite of the vagaries of commercial success, Dickens was always true, in larger matters and in details of character drawing and style, to his idiosyncratic conception of things. And his ideas and their development became public almost as soon as he had them.

A strongly marked feature of this phase of Dickens's life, and one that would last until he died, was the craving for movement and escape, even a sort of hiding out. The ostensible reason for getting away was often frustration at the interference of business and social engagements in the completion of work, but his penchant for travel was so consistent that it is not always clear who or what he was trying to get away from. In an effort to get away from London and England, he took his family to Boulogne for the summer; in an effort to get away from his family, he took a long trip to France and Switzerland with friends in the fall; as soon as he settled in a place, he went on excursions to see the sights. Ackroyd points out that Dickens frequently took rooms where he could finish projects and find some privacy, and from those rooms he frequently took long walks. It is tempting, but risky, of course, to apply diagnoses, such as bipolar disorder, that are current in our time, to persons living in earlier times, and certainly Victorians as a group believed in effort and in making one's way by dint of personal force, especially masculine personal force. But even his fellow Victorians were exhausted by Dickens's restless productivity. Dickens himself was exhausted by it—in May 1853, as he was nearing the end of *Bleak House,* he came down with an agonizing kidney ailment, similar to ailments he had had as a boy and reminiscent of the problems that killed his father. In spite of the pain and the rudimentary medical care, he was back at work in six days. Whether we can diagnose Dickens or not, at least we may say, from the evidence of his activities, his letters, and his works, that he was not at peace, and that there are not even any images of peace to be found. A good life is a busy one; an idle life is both boring and morally suspect. Rest is something ever sought, never found, only occasionally imposed by illness. If every marriage is a belief system, and if one spouse usually dictates the terms of the belief system, then the evidence was growing stronger every day that Catherine was unable to maintain her part in the Dickens family mythology. The reserves of energy that Charles could call upon at will, even when ill, were not available to Catherine. But it must be said that sustaining ten pregnancies and several miscarriages in sixteen years, along with many house movings, social engagements, and long trips, is a task that few modern women would even consider, much less be able to manage.

In January 1854, some six months after the completion of *Bleak House,* Dickens realized that the sales of *Household Words* had fallen precipitously. Bradbury and Evans asked him to compose another serial novel, and he at once began *Hard Times.* The first number appeared on April 1. The immediate inspiration for this shortest of Dickens's novels seems to have been a twenty-three-week-old millworkers' strike in Preston, where Dickens traveled for a look; he then wrote a long piece about the strike for *Household Words* at the beginning of February. Dickens had a long-standing interest in working conditions and workers' protests—he had, of course, touched on lower-class unrest in *Barnaby Rudge* and had intended to write about factories in *Nicholas Nickleby.* He set out his principles clearly in his essay: "that into the relations between employers and employed, as into all the relations in this life, there must enter something of feeling and sentiment; something of mutual explanation, forbearance, and consideration . . . otherwise those relations are wrong and rotten to the core and will never bear sound fruit." His general view of a just society as one marked by the recognition of the dignity and worth of every individual continued to express itself with regard to what seemed to be the purest economic issue, and indeed, the opinion he quotes in his essay from a Preston workers' bill, that the employers "in times of good trade and general prosperity, wrung from their labour a California of gold, which is now being used to crush those who created it," would in our century be read as an expression of the standard Marxist labor theory of value. Dickens's further remarks show that he did not understand this but saw the issue entirely as a matter of relationship. And, indeed, when he novelizes his ideas in *Hard Times,* he can make of them only a depiction of a series of failed relationships between individuals. Mr. Bounderby and Mr. Gradgrind, mill owner and educator, both fail in their responsibilities to their workers, wives, children, and students. They abuse their power, not out of intentional unkindness or natural evil, but out of ideology and ignorance. Those they are supposed to direct, and who turn to them for guidance, receive pat ideas, egocentric bluster, or dry theory. Tom Gradgrind and Louisa are provided with no moral compass or method for understanding their feelings. Stephen Blackpool is reduced step by step to hopelessness and drudgery. The overarching symbol for all of this is the pall of ugliness, smoke, and pollution cast over Coketown by the factories at the heart of the city.

Dickens was not Marx or Engels. Though he was perhaps as outraged as they were at conditions around him, he was by nature a novelist, not a philosopher or a political economist or a revolutionary. Novels privilege the idiosyncrasies of individuals and can demonstrate larger ideas only by having characters work them out through action and contemplation. The narrator may attempt to extrapolate the ideas symbolically, or even to address the reader about them, as Dickens does rather more often in *Hard Times* (rather like Mrs. Stowe, who does the same thing in *Uncle Tom's Cabin*) than he had in previous novels, but the requirement of organizing the material by maintaining clear distinctions between characters means that groups never really come alive in novels—uniformity, crowds, and mass movements disintegrate in the linearity of prose. The novelist's eye can never work successfully as a wide-angle lens but must always move precisely from particular to particular. A novel such as *Hard Times,* where the characters are acting as examples of ideas, always has the air of a cautionary tale or a parable and relies upon a set of beliefs shared between author and readers. The very brevity of *Hard Times* was a challenge to its commercial success because rather than developing his ideas incrementally, by a kind of stealthy inertia or narrative weight, the author expresses them openly. As it happened, Dickens's ideas about education and the proper relations between Capital and Labor were not generally shared, the comic qualities of the novel were not widely appreciated, and *Hard Times* was a failure.

Nevertheless, the novel came to appeal far more to later critics and is perhaps better known as a representative example of Dickens's work in our day than it was in his. As with

Bleak House, modern readers have accepted social criticism as one of the proper uses of novelistic art; in addition, the darkness of Dickens's vision of Coketown coincides more with our own opinions of the ecological and social destructiveness of the Industrial Revolution. Novels since *Hard Times* that have expanded upon and reiterated some of its ideas have helped modern readers share them enough so that they can fade into the background and the characters, who are actually quite entertaining, can emerge.

Dickens always showed an eagerness to contemplate his own situation by fictionalizing it and giving it to one of his characters, sometimes one who was like him (à la David Copperfield) and sometimes one who was quite unlike him (à la Mr. Dick, in the same novel, who is always writing assiduously, but is deeply frustrated that he can't prevent King Charles's head from intruding into his manuscript—perhaps the most perfect image in literature of how a writer comes back and back again to the same concerns in spite of, or because of, how hard he tries to avoid them). In *Hard Times,* Dickens endows the workman Stephen Blackpool, a man otherwise entirely unlike himself, with a burdensome marriage and a wish to divorce. Stephen consults Bounderby, whose answer indicates that Dickens has done some research on the subject: "Why, you'd have to go to Doctors' Commons with a suit, and you'd have to go to a court of Common Law with a suit, and you'd have to get an Act of Parliament to enable you to marry again, and it would cost you . . . I suppose from a thousand to fifteen hundred pound . . . perhaps twice the money." Stephen, of course, earns only a few shillings per week. *Hard Times,* composed in weekly installments like *The*

Old Curiosity Shop, is open and revealing of Dickens's state of mind in much the same way. His demons are no longer grotesque, and the fearsome world is no longer so mysterious and strange; rather, it is all too ugly and factual, peopled by those whose imaginations have been starved rather than perverted. But as with *The Old Curiosity Shop,* Dickens is unable to embody a redemption for any of his characters. Both novels seem to assert that the world, whatever it is made of, cannot be lived in. The longer, more carefully composed novels are never quite this hopeless.

Torment is not uncommon in the lives of novelists and in the lives of nineteenth-century novelists seems to have been the rule rather than the exception. Thackeray's wife was irredeemably insane; George Eliot lived out of wedlock with G. H. Lewes, whose wife continued to produce children with other men; Charlotte Brontë watched her sisters die of tuberculosis and her brother perish of alcoholism before herself dying in childbirth at forty-one; George Sand, Nikolai Gogol, Feodor Dostoevsky, and Leo Tolstoy all lived lives that to us seem dramatic, strenuous, and even tragic, beset in some cases by debt, in others by illness, madness, loss, grief, political imprisonment. The onus was on them, nevertheless, to produce an art that was acceptable to the middle classes and, above all, respectable. With the passing of patronage and the broadening of an author's audience, his or her social function (and therefore his or her source of income) shifted. Every novel seeks to entertain—beginning with the rise of the novel as a literary form, the fact that novels entertain was invoked as an essential criticism: young persons read novels rather than, say, sermons and thereby failed to improve their morals or their stock of knowledge—but the novel also has to enlighten, in order to attain and then maintain respectability. Novelists themselves, and Dickens was one of the first, understood at once the power of the form to reflect the world of the nineteenth century back to its citizens in a new and instructive way, but there were limits to what the middle classes were willing to ponder. Some novelists were more daring than others—Harriet Beecher Stowe, for example, touches pretty firmly on marriage and sexuality, as well as upon slavery, in *Uncle Tom's Cabin*. Dickens's attacks on the structure of English society were bolder than those of his contemporaries, who tended to focus on individuals. What novelists could not do, except by indirection, was reveal their personal torments in their art, especially if their personal torments were not quite respectable, and few torments are. For Dickens, whose purchase on his own middle-class life was always open to challenge, and whose expressed ideals of happiness and goodness were typical Victorian domestic ones, the contradiction between outward appearance and inner reality was especially dangerous.

Dickens considered himself a reliable witness to, and an authority upon, social conditions of his time. Not only did he expend a great deal of energy informing himself, he also was in the habit of expressing his opinion and acting upon it. But as his critique broadened and darkened, he became less and less capable of putting it over. His style, or "genius," as everyone called it, which was the essential and unchangeable feature of his vision, never failed to remind readers of his peculiarity. The lightheartedness and humor of earlier works had made a comprehensible bridge between the world as it is and the world as it should be, and he had successfully embodied redemption through love, friendship, celebration, plenty, laughter, forgiveness, pleasure, character improvement, and the punishment of evil. In the 1850s, however, he no longer believed in improvement. One factor was the Crimean War of 1854–1855, the conduct of which exposed the incompetence of the government so that Dickens wrote his friend Mrs. Watson, "I feel as if the world had been pushed back 500 years." He strongly felt that every official was shirking responsibility, as he wrote in an essay in August 1856: "The power of Nobody is becoming so enormous in England. . . . The hand which this surprising person had in the late war is amazing to consider. It was he who left the tents behind, who left the baggage behind, who chose the worst possible ground for encampments, who provided no means of transport, who killed the horses, who paralyzed the commissariat, who knew nothing of the business he professed to know and monopolized, who decimated the English army." After developing this theme for several pages, he concludes, "Nobody has done more harm in this single generation than Everybody can mend in ten generations."

The war served only to confirm the contempt for Parliament he had felt first during his years reporting parliamentary speeches in the early 1830s. He always believed that the House of Commons was corrupted by self-interest, bribery, and collusion. He knew after twenty years of charitable endeavor that the alleviation of unsanitary public health conditions, for example, or the successful prosecution of a war was a public function, to be undertaken by the government in behalf of the citizens, but he saw no evidence that the British ruling class had any desire or will to do its duty.

But the form of redemption Dickens represented in the public mind, and certainly in his own mind, redemption in domestic companionship and happiness, no longer seemed real to the man himself. Though he treated Catherine with consideration and courtesy at this point, in January 1855, he wrote Forster, "Why is it, that as with poor David, a sense comes always crushing on me now, when I fall into low spirits, as of one happiness I have missed in life and one friend and companion I have never made?" He had given David Copperfield Agnes Wickfield, and he had given Allan Woodcourt Esther Summerson. He could imagine the sort of woman that a busy, benevolent, ambitious, energetic, and introspective man might love as a friend, companion, and wife, but he did not have that woman in his own life, and it is altogether possible that the authorial act of matching his alter ego, David, with Agnes exacerbated his sense of what he was missing. It was one thing for his fictional stand-in, John Jarndyce, to accept the role of kindly, detached guardian to his extended family; it was quite a different thing for the author himself, a man who fathered ten children in sixteen years. We may easily extrapolate Dickens's ardor in every other area of his life to his sexual passions, although all the evidence is that however he felt, he had conducted himself up to this point with stern propriety. Nevertheless, within weeks of his confession to Forster, his longings were strangely answered through a letter from his first love, Maria Winter, née Beadnell.

By his own admission, Dickens had been in love with, and obsessed by, Maria Beadnell for some four years, between the ages of seventeen and twenty-one, while he was working as a law clerk and shorthand parliamentary reporter. She was the daughter of a banker, and it has remained unknown how he first made her acquaintance or came to be accepted, at least provisionally, as an admirer, of which Maria had several. They met and also exchanged letters, some of them in secret after her father disapproved of the connection. In May 1833, Dickens declared his passionate love one last time, but her response was cool, and he parted from her. He met George Hogarth in 1834 and Catherine sometime between September and December of that year. There seemed always to be the sense that his regard for Catherine did not carry the passion of his attachment to Maria Beadnell. At any rate, when Mrs. Winter, now forty-four, wrote him, he responded warmly and at length, recalling his earlier feelings with great freshness. In their renewed correspondence, to quote the narrator of *Hard Times,* with reference to Louisa and James Harthouse, "He . . . established a confidence with her from which her husband was excluded." Not to mention his wife.

Dickens's first letter to Mrs. Winter is worth quoting at length, if only to show how his mind worked:

As I was reading by the fire last night, a handful of notes was laid down on my table. I looked them over, and, recognizing the writing of no private friend, let them lie there and went back to my book. But I found my mind curiously disturbed, and wandering away through so many years to early times of my life, that I was quite perplexed to account for it. There was nothing in what I had been reading, or immediately thinking about to awaken such a train of thought, and at last it came into my head that it must have been suggested by something in the look of one of those letters. So I turned them over again—and suddenly the remembrance of your hand came upon me with an influence that I cannot express to you. Three or four and twenty years vanished like a dream, and I opened it with the touch of my young friend David Copperfield when he was in love.

There was something so busy and so pleasant in your letter—so true and cheerful and frank and affectionate—that I read on with perfect delight until I came to your mention of your two little girls. In the unsettled state of my thoughts, the existence of these dear children appeared such a prodigious phenomenon, that I was included to suspect myself of being out of my mind until it occurred to me that perhaps I had nine children of my own!

Dickens then goes on in a somewhat less personal vein, but six days later, he wrote her again from Paris:

There are things that I have locked up in my own breast and that I never thought to bring out any more. But when I find myself writing "all to yourself," how can I forbear to let as much light in upon them as will shew you that they are there still! If the most innocent, the most ardent, and the most disinterested days of my life had you for their sun—as indeed they had—and if I know that the Dream I lived in did me good, refined my heart, and made me patient and persevering, and if the Dream were all of you—as

God knows it was—how can I receive a confidence of you, and return it, and make a feint of blotting all this out.

Dickens's remarkable grace as a correspondent combined with his eagerness clearly gave Mrs. Winter something to think about. We can guess what when we read in his next letter, dated from Tavistock House six days later, "When you say you are 'toothless, fat, old and ugly' (which I don't believe), I fly away to the house in Lombard Street, which is pulled down . . . and see you in a sort of raspberry dress with a little black trimming at the top—black velvet it seems to be made of—cut in vandykes—an immense number of vandykes—with my boyish heart pinned like a captured butterfly on every one of them." He goes on to discuss the arrangements for the meeting (which included Catherine and Mr. Winter) and to urge that he and Mrs. Winter might meet first alone because "I feel it, as it were, so necessary to our being at ease."

But the meeting was not a success. Mrs. Winter was as she described herself and, in addition, extremely talkative. Dickens quickly disembarrassed himself of further intimacy, but his April letter to her, making excuses for missing an engagement, is revealing. By this time, Dickens was in the throes of planning *Little Dorrit:*

You have never seen it before you, or lived with it, or had occasion to care about it, and you cannot have the necessary consideration for it. "It is only half an hour"—"It is only an afternoon"—"It is only an evening"—people say to me over and over again—but they don't know that it is impossible to command oneself to any stipulated and set disposal of five minutes, or that the mere consciousness of an engagement will sometimes worry a day away. These are the penalties paid for writing books. Whoever is devoted to an Art must be content to deliver himself wholly up to it, and to find his recompense in it.

Dickens embarrassed himself with Mrs. Winter and then compounded his embarrassment by writing her into *Little Dorrit* as the foolish and garrulous but kindhearted Flora. He exposed himself to his friends, but also to himself. Later in the year he wrote to Forster rather defensively, "I don't quite apprehend what you mean by my overrating the strength of the feeling of five-and-twenty years ago. If you mean of my own feeling, and will only think what the desperate intensity of my nature is . . . that it excluded every other idea from my mind for four years . . . and that I went at it with a determination to overcome all the difficulties, which fairly lifted me up into that newspaper life, and floated me away over a hundred men's heads . . . nothing can exaggerate that. I have positively stood amazed at myself ever since!"

Bleak House sold well, and *Hard Times* raised the circulation and profits of *Household Words,* but after a visit to England in 1855, Nathaniel Hawthorne remarked, "Dickens is evidently not liked nor thought well of by his literary brethren—at least, the most eminent of them, whose reputation might interfere with his. Thackeray is much more to their tastes." Bad reviews abounded of both books, though Dickens said that he never read reviews. In this, Dickens's life and work continued to be of a piece and continued to express his unique place in

English society. He simply did not fit in. In the first place, he was too imposing and had been around too long—predating almost every other serious author of his own age by years or decades. His worldview formed part of the raw material from which they made their own and which they were required to differ from in order to establish their authorial identities. His well-known generosity and helpfulness had two sides—he encouraged and promoted the work of others, in so doing promoting the respectability of authorship itself, which was important to him, but he also had very particular views about what was good and entertaining and what the role of authors in society should be. Unsurprisingly, he was his own best example of the right sort of thing: socially engaged, entertaining, lively, and fanciful. He often called himself "the Inimitable," and indeed he was exactly that. But for that very reason, he didn't fit in.

Additionally, as Dickens grew more radical in his political views (and more idiosyncratic—we should not interpret him as the sort of left liberal we know today—he was racist, imperialist, sometimes anti-Semitic, a believer in harsh prison conditions, and distrustful of trade unions), he divided himself more and more from his fellow novelists. How do we make sense of this? It is important to note, to begin with, that the literary world of Victorian England was small and personal. Writers and editors knew each other, often socialized and worked together, and published each other's works to a degree that simply no longer obtains even in England, where the literary world is significantly more interconnected than that of the United States. Obviously, however, no one had any power to restrict the publication of Dickens's work. He was his own editor, and virtually his own publisher, and his relationship to his audience continued unimpeded.

All they could really do was complain. Charlotte Brontë complained that she disliked Dickens's "extravagance" (but neither was *Jane Eyre* to his taste). George Eliot, whose first two books Dickens praised in very kind letters, considered his work shallow and melodramatic. Thackeray, Dickens's some-time friend, admired several of Dickens's works, especially *Dombey and Son* and *A Christmas Carol,* but felt a strong ri-valry toward Dickens, which, it must have been irritating for Thackeray to sense, Dickens hardly noticed. (Dickens judged Thackeray on how he conducted himself as an author, not, it appears, on what he wrote.) Trollope called Dickens "Mr. Popular Sentiment." In fact, it appears that Dickens consid-ered his own literary tastes to be private ones. He may have liked or disliked certain books, but he always supported the social role of authorship and the success of authors in general. They had to denigrate him, but he did not have to denigrate them and, indeed, seems to have understood that his power to promote or denigrate the work of any individual was enor-mous and should be used with caution. He did not, for ex-ample, review books. As an editor, he made work available. As a famous author, he did not make his judgments, especially negative ones, well known.

These most famous authors were not the only ones. There were many working writers and critics whose work has no modern currency, and they, too, all had their opinions of Dickens and his set. Generally that opinion was negative, based partly on the sorts of things published in *Household Words* and partly on the class origins and personal habits of the writers. Dickens had always preferred to surround himself with self-made men from backgrounds similar to his, to dress loudly, to go out to all sorts of theatrical entertainments. He didn't fit in.

He made fun. He made fun of the Civil Service, he made fun of the courts of Chancery, he made fun of the aristocracy and the factory owners and the bankers and the managerial class. He made fun of educators and moneylenders and women who married for money. He made fun of Parliament. He made fun of selfishness and self-interest of all kinds. He made fun of all sorts of religious types, but especially Evangelicals. He made fun of feckless young men and libidinous old men and government officials like beadles. But more important, his mind did not work by means of analytical sifting of premises and data, or through a refined analysis of motive and moral reckoning, as, say, George Eliot's mind worked. Dickens's mind worked symbolically. He apprehended the world through figures that were endowed with meaning. Objects come alive, and people become mechanical. His style invariably expresses a worldview that seems almost unmediated by normal reasonable discourse, as if there is no objective reality, only a subjective reality in which meanings present themselves in terms of vivid figures, come into conflict with one another, and shift. Eliot, whose art depends on the notion of characters living in an objective world that they must come to understand through experience and reasoning, whose mysteries are hidden in gradations of motive and action, would of course not appreciate the terror and joy of Dickens's highly distinct subjectivity. But Dickens appeals to that part of the reader that recognizes that much is left undiscussed by reasonable discourse, that people and institutions often do populate our inner lives not as who they are but as what they mean to us, and that we often do not see them whole and complex, but simple and strange. This view, of course, has an affinity with childhood, as Dickens had an affinity with childhood, but it also has an affinity with many states of consciousness throughout life, including madness or obsession and exalted states of love or spiritual transcendence. That Dickens submerged into his style many good, useful, and humane ideas is a testament to the fact that his vision did not prevent him from living and working in the world, but simply intensified his experience of it. As he said to Forster, "Only think what the desperate intensity of my nature is."

Hard Times was published in August 1854, and Dickens once again took a short break from writing novels, though he continued to write for *Household Words*. Amateur theatricals were consuming more of his time, and in December, as a charity fund-raiser, he tried a new thing, reading *A Christmas Carol* and *The Cricket on the Hearth* aloud to an audience in Birmingham for the cause of workingmen's education. He had plenty of experience reading the Christmas books aloud; each of them had been introduced to his friends in this way, and all of them had gone over well—when he read *The Chimes* aloud, he reported William Macready "undisguisedly sobbing, and crying on the sofa," and his painter friend, Daniel Maclise (who did a sketch of the occasion), said, "There was not a dry eye in the house." Dickens read three nights in Birmingham, the third night to an audience of two thousand workingmen and -women who each paid sixpence for tickets. When he came home, thrilled with both the experience and his reception, he told his editor at *Household Words,* W. H. Wills, according to Wills, "If they *will* have him he will do it." The idea was not to make money by it, as yet. There was still a sense of impropriety attached to the idea of an author performing in public, but with his love of and talent for the stage, Dickens certainly was drawn to the idea if only, for now, as a mode of raising money for good causes.

When December 1855 came around, Dickens set up several more charitable readings, one in Reading, one in Sherborne, and one in Bradford that attracted 3,700 people, followed by another in London. He read *A Christmas Carol* each time and used the story and the time of year and the occasions to promote the sort of openhearted generosity that had always been important to him. But the moneymaking possibilities were obvious and the temptation to exploit them growing stronger. As important, though, was Dickens's palpable sense of his own popularity and power. It was one thing to act in a play or a farce, in character and often speaking the words of another author. It was quite different to say his own words, passing through the personae of characters he himself had created, giving voice and action to his own inner life. His daughter Mamie once reported having an illness as a child and spending the day in his study while he was working: "He suddenly jumped from his chair and rushed to a mirror which hung near, and in which I could see the reflection of some extraordinary facial contortions which he was making. He returned rapidly to his desk, wrote furiously for a few moments, and then went again to the mirror. The facial pantomime was resumed, and then turning toward but evidently not seeing me, he began talking in a low voice."

Dickens's children were now eighteen, seventeen, fifteen, fourteen, eleven, nine, eight, six, and nearly three, seven boys and two girls. He was a strict and orderly father, who insisted upon neatness and quiet, especially while he was working, but who also had a knack for talking to young children and eliciting confidences in return. Music, dancing, and performing were a significant part of the Dickens family life. It seems clear that he did not want his children to repeat any of his early experiences of poverty, family instability, or street life; they were educated and prepared for a typical English middle-class adulthood. He did complain that they weren't especially ambitious or hardworking, at least in comparison with the energy he had brought to making his way at their age. They were not raised on tales of their father's youth; during a Christmas game toward the end of his life, when most of his children were in their twenties and thirties, Dickens said, "Warren's Blacking, Thirty Strand," and none of the children had any idea what he meant. Now, in 1855, it was getting to be the time when the older children would need to be provided with careers, and Charley, whom Miss Coutts had sent for a while to Eton, seemed particularly unsettled. He went to Germany for two years, to study banking, but Dickens wrote apologetically to Miss Coutts that Charley had "less fixed purpose and energy than [I] could have supposed in a child of mine." Thackeray's daughters were friends of Dickens's daughters, and Thackeray commented on their elaborate style of dress. Catherine remarked to a friend that

Dickens always liked the children best when they were babies and toddlers. At any rate, his restlessness seems to have been partly a result of his populous household. He often traveled alone or with male friends, both for work and for sightseeing, and 1855 was no exception. He spent two weeks in Paris with Wilkie Collins in February, then took the family to Folkestone in July. In November, he moved the family to Paris, where they stayed until May 1856, although Dickens himself returned to England from time to time. From June through August, Dickens summered with his family in Boulogne.

He was now writing *Little Dorrit,* though it was not going at all well, and his letters to Forster were full of frustration and anxiety. His initial ideas were thematic ones—building upon his success with *Bleak House* and his views of the conduct of the Crimean War, he wanted to explore the notion of "Nobody's Fault," which was the original title of the novel. But it was evidently not productive, because though he began thinking in January and expected by May to start publishing in November, in August and September he was still contemplating starting over. The novel begins with Rigaud and Cavaletto in jail in Marseilles, Dickens's first depiction of non-English characters in a setting quite distant in both geography and ambience from London. It is distinctly not what Mrs. Gaskell would have called "Dickensy," and when the English characters enter in chapter 2, they are not very Dickensy, either. In particular, Arthur Clennam is almost a blank— quiet, colorless, already resigned, and even beaten down by his upbringing and his life in the Far East (which is not evoked at all). A few other minor characters are introduced, but the novel doesn't really gain any energy until chapter 6, when the scene moves to the Marshalsea Debtors' Prison, where the eponymous Little Dorrit lives with her father, brother, and sister. Dickens's purpose from the beginning, one that he mentioned to Forster, was to depict ever-tightening connections and relationships among a large cast of characters who at first seem to bump up against each other randomly, like travelers passing together through the same scenes, only to part and bump into one another again later.

Dickens returns to some of the themes he explored in *Dombey and Son,* but now the sources of money are more various than they were in *Dombey.* The essential source is productive creativity. Property and rents and trade have a more problematic moral character; how they are managed dictates what good they are. Banking requires prudence, exactness, and benevolence but is not inherently corrupt. Investment or speculation is inherently corrupt. Dickens also explores the uses money is put to and finds them generally bad. In *Little Dorrit,* prosperity itself is almost a guarantee that wealth will be put to bad use. The primary example of this is that when poor and in debt, the members of the Dorrit family live generally in kindly intimacy with one another, but when raised to sudden wealth, kindness, service, and even expressions of love are considered humiliating. Who pays, who is supported, and whether these arrangements are legitimate is a constant concern of the novel.

Love circulates like money but is mostly powerless against the wholesale commodification of social and domestic relationships. In *Little Dorrit,* Dickens shows a world made up of debtors and cheats, among whom one or two decent, hardworking, self-effacing figures move silently, often dishonored, rarely regarded, and only at the last minute, when almost all hope is gone, rewarded.

Dickens's vision in *Little Dorrit* is not only an exceptionally dark view of human nature, it is specifically a dark view of British society and of the effects of British social and economic structure upon British citizens. The Circumlocution Office and the Barnacles and Stiltstalkings who inhabit it are pervasive in both government and society, making sure that no business that might promote the common good is ever done, while all relationships are rendered false. The Circumlocution principle is shown to be more powerful and important even than the Chancery court, in *Bleak House,* because while Chancery court touches upon all aspects of British society, it does not define them, as the Circumlocution Office docs in *Little Dorrit*. There are only two refuges from it, exile and prison.

The plot of *Little Dorrit* is overelaborate and creaky. The two halves, the first of which follows the Dorrits in their poverty and the second of which follows them in their wealth, have a profound simplicity that makes William and Fanny two of Dickens's most complex and ruthlessly drawn characters. But their effect is undermined by the convolutions of the Clennam plot, which involves Arthur's long-lost unknown mother, who died mad, a twin for Jeremiah Flintwinch, the melodramatic recuperation of Mrs. Clennam, and the literal collapse of her house. Rigaud/Blandois is simultaneously overdrawn and uninteresting—too ubiquitous and without even the most minimal complexity or fun. Even Bounderby, the villain of *Hard Times,* is fun. Even Uriah Heep is a little fun. Rigaud/Blandois tempts the reader to skip his parts from the beginning to the end.

Dickens was frequently criticized in his own time for not portraying his characters with much complexity or depth. George Eliot, for example, wrote in 1856 that "he failed to give us their psychological character." But many Dickens characters are beautifully layered. Almost invariably, though, these, like Dora or Flora Finching or William Dorrit, are his voluble ones, and they reveal themselves through their own dialogue or monologue. Flora Finching is a particularly appropriate example of several aspects of Dickens's working style. For one thing, she was based on Mrs. Winter, whose talkativeness Dickens had found so offputting in the spring of 1856. At first, the portrayal of her seems cruel, and must have seemed so to Mrs. Winter herself, who, Dickens was well aware, read all of his work attentively. She is not only fat, she is flirtatious and foolish. Arthur finds her repugnant and his former feeling unaccountable. She drinks. But Dickens gives free rein to her tongue, and many of her idea associations are funny and smart; she also shows considerable self-knowledge. She is kindhearted. By the end of the novel, she is one of the most endearing characters, perhaps the only truly endearing character, who clearly understands her failures, her father's faults, and the difficulties of Mr. F.'s aunt, but on the whole chooses to make the best of things in a world where most of the characters choose quite the opposite. Dickens understood intuitively that speech is a form of narrative, wherein the speaker narrates his or her own life to others as well as to him- or herself. He anticipates in this not only Freud, but also

Bakhtin and other theorists of the novel who maintain that the uniqueness of the novel as an art form derives from the clash and the complementarity of many voices. Dickens was also wonderful at the sort of indirect discourse where the author in the narrative voice appropriates various languages that occur in the general discourse, sometimes for whole paragraphs and sometimes for only a phrase. In chapter 24, when Amy takes dinner at Flora's, Mr. F.'s aunt is not at the table. She "was, for the time, laid up in ordinary in her chamber," that is, like a noncommissioned ship that is still afloat. Often Dickens goes on at some length in this manner. When the Plornishes visit Arthur in prison, the narrator notes, "Mr. Plornish amiably growled, in his philosophical but not quite lucid manner, that there was ups, you see, and there was downs. It was in vain to ask why ups, why downs; there they was, you know." This form of discourse often functions metaphorically, but its main effect is to widen the world of the novel, to refer to and incorporate a huge variety of colloquial forms of speech, and to reinforce the idea that the novel mimics life. That appropriating, mimicking, and delighting in the plentiful varieties of English speech was one of Dickens's signal traits, all of his acquaintances agreed upon, and he was perfectly alive to how speech and characteristic action revealed character.

The other side of this trait, though, is that he was often drawn to portray his positive characters as quiet, repressed, or self-effacing, in contrast with the parading egos of morally neutral or negative characters. Dickens's final image of Arthur and Amy swallowed up in the roar of the city not only portrays their unique fate, it also encapsulates the effect of their portrayals throughout the novel. The clamor of the surrounding personalities has served as a continual distraction from the blanks where their personalities should be. If we give Dickens credit for intentionally delineating them as he does, then at this point in his career, his art is asserting that personality *is* a form of ego, and, as with *The Old Curiosity Shop,* there is no way to exist expressively in the world without partaking of its egomania. What Eliot often did well that Dickens did not do was anatomize her quiet characters, such as Rosamund Vincy in *Middlemarch.* Understanding layers of intention and desire beneath a quiet exterior was one of Eliot's interests and a strength of her writing—her characters are often portrayed in solitude, where they are free to reveal (or the author is free to reveal for them) their true natures. Dickens's characters reveal their true natures through social intercourse. He has not got much access to them if they hold themselves apart from others.

Little Dorrit achieved excellent sales. The first numbers sold around forty thousand copies each, and though by the last numbers sales had declined to just over thirty thousand, still that was much higher than *David Copperfield* and nearly as high as *Bleak House.* Some critics liked it (George Bernard Shaw said "it was a more seditious book than *Das Kapital,*" a definite compliment), others were offended, others found it too drawn out. Forster did not like it, faulting its failures of invention and its labored quality. It ran from the end of 1855 through mid-1857 and was published in volume form in June.

In 1856, during the writing of *Little Dorrit,* John Forster, who was the same age as Dickens, forty-four, married a wealthy widow, certainly to the surprise and somewhat to the dismay of his friends, including Dickens. Forster and his new wife immediately set up rather elaborate housekeeping in the heart of the very society that Dickens was busily excoriating in his novel; Dickens was a bit disapproving. Forster had grown more politically conservative since 1850, precisely during the time when Dickens was growing more radical. Dickens still wrote openly to Forster of his most important concerns, but Forster was not as supportive as he had been. As a result, Dickens's letters took on a note of defensive explanation that makes them especially informative. Forster had his own opinions about marriage, now that he was married, and his opinions grew out of just that sort of compatibility of abilities and views that Dickens missed in his own—he may have disapproved of what marriage into society had done to the old Forster, but he would certainly have noticed that Forster had achieved something, through luck or good judgment, that he himself missed very much.

Also during the writing of *Little Dorrit,* Dickens had realized yet another dream, which was to buy Gad's Hill Place, a large house near Chatham, in Kent, the very house that he and his father had often admired when Dickens was a boy. Dickens wrote of its purchase to a friend, "I happened to be walking past . . . with my sub-editor of *Household Words* when I said to him: 'You see that house? It has always a curious interest for me, because when I was a small boy down in these parts I thought it the most beautiful house (I suppose because of its famous old cedar trees) ever seen. And my poor father used to bring me to look at it, and used to say that if I ever grew up to be a clever man perhaps I might own that house or another such house . . .' We came back to town and my friend went out to dinner. Next morning he came in great excitement, and said, 'It is written that you were to have that house at Gad's Hill Place. The lady I had allotted to me to take down to dinner yesterday began to speak of that neighborhood, 'You know it?' I said, 'I have been there today.' 'Oh, yes,' she said. 'I know it very well, I was a child there, in the house they call Gad's Hill Place. My father was the rector, and lived there many years. He has just died, has left it to me, and I want to sell it.'" Dickens, of course, could not resist. The house had associations not only with his childhood, but also with Shakespeare—Falstaff has a famous scene in *Henry IV* that takes place at Gad's Hill.

Dickens's restlessness infected every facet of his life. In the two years between June 1855 and June 1857, he had bought two new houses, lived at Folkestone, Paris, Boulogne, and London, and traveled besides for speeches and business. His level of activity, with writing, editing, reading in public, and managing the lives of his children, was higher than ever. His enthusiasm for amateur acting and play production was immense; he supervised the production of, and took roles in, six plays and farces, all of which were put on in the small theater at Tavistock House. The evidence of his writings, his frenzy of activities, and his letters about both personal and political subjects show that he was approaching a crisis and that he himself had identified the crisis as a domestic one. Dickens's life continued to look strangely modern, ruled by a need for freedom of all kinds and increasingly impatient with the typical patterns of his Victorian world.

CHAPTER FIVE

WILKIE COLLINS, Dickens's friend and fellow writer, had written a play called *The Frozen Deep*. As always, Dickens was more than an adviser in its composition—almost a collaborator, though Collins's name was listed as author. When the play went into production, at the end of 1856, for Twelfth Night performances at Tavistock House, Dickens became the director, star, stage manager, theater owner, and moving force. The play took its theme from an Arctic expedition of 1845, the Franklin expedition to find the Northwest Passage, in which all were lost, with some allegations of cannibalism. Dickens played the leader of the expedition, Richard Wardour, whom Collins had envisioned as the villain, but whom Dickens rewrote and played as an angry, complex, and self-sacrificing man "perpetually seeking and never finding true affection." Dickens rehearsed, sometimes in company and sometimes alone, all through November and December 1856. According to Ackroyd, he kept his monologues to himself, no doubt knowing that he was about to create a sensation, and then, in January, he allowed reviewers to come to the performances along with the invited guests; they testified to the sensation he succeeded in creating. The entire audience was deeply affected; Collins reportedly said, "This is an awful thing!" One reviewer noted the "irrational" depths of Dickens's performance (which we may interpret in a Freudian way as seeming to come from the id or the unconscious, or in a Jungian way as seeming to come from the collective unconscious, or in a more traditional way as seeming to carry a force beyond that of a single individual, as being "inspired," a state Dickens was entirely familiar with). The requirements of the evening's program meant that Dickens had to change almost at once for his part in the farce, "Uncle John," but afterward, during the dancing, one of the ladies present reported that Dickens asked her to waltz and she "was whirled around almost to giddiness." Dickens had found a way to express his feelings about his life in his own voice and with his own body, rather than through the medium of a character in a novel. The expression of his anger and his disappointment and his love for the woman Richard Wardour gives up to his rival in the play had the powerful effect of both arousing and relieving his generally repressed feelings about his marital situation.

The lives of novelists, and actors, too, are marked by bouts of emotion and changes of circumstances—love affairs, divorces, outbursts of all kinds—that supposedly contrast with the lives of citizens with more traditional employments. This flux is conventionally seen as evidence of instability on the part of artists and ascribed to wounds of childhood, or artistic temperament, or selfishness. But the true pattern, I think, is evident in Dickens's relationship to his work and is most evident from the inception of *David Copperfield,* in 1849, to the end of his life. Every novelist brings some knowledge of dramatic states of mind to his writing. If he or she had no such knowledge, then he or she would have no business with, and no interest in, novels or drama, since both rely on the depiction of those states for narrative or dramatic interest. Audiences and readers want something to happen, and writers are ready to portray some of the things that can happen. Often this knowledge does have its root in the experience of the artist, though as frequently it has its origins in sensitive and eager observation (both of these were certainly true of Dickens). But the experience of writing about and depicting these dramatic incidents is at least as important as their origins, because the novelist bodies them forth, comments upon them, reacts to them; he learns from them and gives them both form and meaning, rather like, in a simpler way, expressing anger in words sometimes relieves feelings and sometimes exacerbates them. What might have remained inchoate becomes specific through making a narrative of it in a way that is analogous to psychotherapy. The novelist, unlike the patient, defines his story as fiction and therefore retains at least some distance from it, but he nevertheless learns to interpret it. Often it loses its power over him, as Dickens came to terms with his months in the blacking factory after giving them to David Copperfield. But he may also learn things about his true state of mind that might have remained shadowy had he not embodied them. In *David Copperfield* and every subsequent novel, Dickens created ideal heroines—Agnes Wickfield, Esther Summerson, Sissy Jupe and Rachael (in *Hard Times*), and Amy Dorrit—who contrasted strongly with his perception of his wife. They were healthy, industrious, intelligent, companionable, slender, unselfish pre-mothers with the strength to withstand circumstances and enter into a kinship with flawed but loving men, several of whom were overt or covert stand-ins for Dickens himself. In every novel they were contrasted with other female characters—Dora, Flora, Lady Dedlock, Louisa—who were not rewarded with male companionship at the end of the novel. And with each novel, Dickens taught himself that he was missing what the characters he wrote about managed to achieve (and what several of the men around him also managed to achieve—his father, whose insolvency frequently aroused Dickens's scorn, was evidently happily married to Dickens's mother for more than forty years in a sort of "I will never leave Mr. Micawber"–type union). Art that has a revelatory effect upon the reader had its first revelatory effect upon the writer; the process of working out the plots and the relationships in an ambitious novel is always a learning process. In Dickens's case, the fact that the novels were published as they were written and the fact that they were so long and multilayered meant that the challenge of maintaining the forward motion along with the integrity of the story and the characters was enormous. What the author knows at the end cannot possibly be the same as what he knew at the beginning, and what he knows has reference to every aspect of his emotional and symbolic life.

Additionally, he has only himself as his guide and judge. The leavening presence of, say, a psychotherapist is not there to mediate the continuous sense of revelation the novelist feels as he gives meaning to his conceptions and feelings. For Dickens, who lived so public a life, there was some index of how far in or out of the mainstream of conventional thinking he was through reviews, sales, and opinions of friends, therefore some potential therapistlike check upon his wildest thoughts, but the feedback was mixed. High sales bolstered his sense of being right; he never read reviews; he had come to discount the opinions of Forster and other close friends. His primary ambition, which was to arouse strong feelings of sympathy and pathos in his audience, was almost invariably realized—at some remove through the novels, with great immediacy through the performances of *The Frozen Deep*. This sympathy he must certainly have interpreted as support or approval, moving him along bit by bit toward acting upon the feelings he had been portraying for so long.

Authors live in a dialogue with their work, and their work is their inner life made concrete. Were they not susceptible to the reality of art, they wouldn't have become authors in the first place. They would naturally be at least as susceptible to the power of their own art as to the power of the art of others, and from the beginning of his career, Dickens's letters attest to his enthusiasm for and belief in every novel he wrote. When he came to the end of *Little Dorrit*, in June 1857, he was ripe for a change. Such a term, however, misstates and slights the state of mind he was in, which was very vulnerable, though his vulnerability was cloaked in his usual wit and activity.

During the later spring of 1857, Hans Christian Andersen visited the Dickens family at Gad's Hill Place. Expected to stay only briefly, Andersen made himself at home for five weeks (after he left, Dickens put a note in the room he had used that read, "Hans Andersen slept in this room for five weeks—which seemed to the family AGES") and noticed, it was said later, that Catherine was unhappy from time to time. The rest of the family did not make him feel especially welcome; the strain may have been caused by him, or he may have imposed himself upon a situation where strain was already being felt. On June 8, Dickens's friend and fellow writer Douglas Jerrold died suddenly. They had known each other for many years; of the two of them, another writer wrote, "Jerrold flies at his enemy like a tiger, and never lets go while there is life in him; while Dickens contents himself by giving him a sound drubbing. Jerrold is most in earnest, but Dickens is more effective." Jerrold left a wife and a daughter, and Dickens immediately began to arrange for some sort of performances or readings to benefit them. The goal was £2,000, a considerable sum that Dickens was confident he could raise. At the end of June, he read *A Christmas Carol* to a large crowd. On July 4, he and his fellow amateurs, who included Georgina Hogarth and his daughters Mamie and Katey in the women's parts, gave a private performance of *The Frozen Deep* for Queen Victoria and her party that was also a great success. Other performances of Collins's play followed, but when it appeared that the planned performances were not going to earn the expected sum (Dickens liked his productions to be both elaborate and perfect; often costs overran projections), Dickens agreed to put on a performance in a large hall in Manchester. When he went to have a look at it, he realized that Georgina and his daughters did not have the skills to project their lines in such a large space, and he asked a friend to recommend some professional actresses.

The Ternan family, who were hired to play the parts, consisted of the mother, Frances, and three daughters, Fanny, Maria, and Ellen. Frances had acted with Charles Macready in various Shakespearean productions and was a serious and respected actress; the father, Thomas, had managed several theaters and was also a specialist in serious theater. He had died not long before, possibly, according to Ackroyd, of the late-stage effects of syphilis. The two older daughters were accomplished actresses, and the addition of the family gave the production the energy it needed, in more ways than one.

Dickens wrote of the effect of the first night's performance, "It was a good thing to have a couple of thousand people all rigid and frozen together in the palm of one's hand . . . and to see the hardened Carpenters at the sides crying and trembling at it. . . ." Even Maria Ternan, experienced though she was, wept as she cradled the dying Richard Wardour (Dickens) in her arms, so that Dickens had to recall her to her professional obligations. Only two performances had been planned, but the play was such a sensation that a third was added. Of his own experiences at Manchester, Dickens later wrote to Collins, "I have never known a moment's peace or content since the last night of 'The Frozen Deep.'"

In September, the Ternans were appearing, during Doncaster race week, at a theater in Doncaster. Dickens arranged a trip with Wilkie Collins for the composition of a piece for *Household Words* to be titled "The Lazy Tour of Two Idle Apprentices." Collins was younger than Dickens, unmarried, and likely to overlook any risky doings, since he himself had considerable experience of the seamier side of Victorian life. They traveled first to Scotland, where Dickens got them into trouble mountain climbing and had to carry the injured Collins down the hillside. Collins's injury, a sprained ankle, did not prevent Dickens from taking him on to Doncaster. There, he was with the Ternans, and Ellen, several times, but what they did can only be inferred from Dickens's letters and writings. All that is known is that Ellen had small parts in plays, that Dickens went out several times, that Dickens was seen at the theater and cheered by the audience, and that he left suddenly, writing in a letter afterward, "The Doncaster unhappiness remains so strong upon me that I can't write, and (waking) can't rest, one minute."

In October, as a result of a dispute, Dickens told Catherine's maid to erect a partition in their bedroom so that he could sleep separately from her. The origin of the dispute remains unclear (though Catherine had frequently expressed jealousy of his feelings for other women, going all the way back to Madame de la Rue, and with good reason), but its result was irrevocable—they never lived as man and wife again, and thenceforth, Dickens seems to have allowed his dislike of her to emerge more and more openly.

Dickens's feelings about the women in his life were invariably strong. What he said of his love for Maria Beadnell, that it was a four-year obsession, applied in degree if not in kind to his feelings about every woman with whom he felt a connection. Sometimes the strong feelings were positive, as for Mary Hogarth, Georgina Hogarth, and his daughters; sometimes they were negative. Over the years he expressed contempt and dislike for his mother, for his wife, and for his wife's mother. In some sense, it does not matter what these women were actually like or how others saw them. After Dickens had endowed them with a particular symbolic meaning, his feelings about them did not admit of contradiction. Everything they did or said just reconfirmed his opinions and intensified his feelings. His work showed that he had ideas about how a woman should be. The ideal women characters, like Esther Summerson and Agnes Wickfield, are balanced by portraits of many decidedly nonideal characters such as Mrs. Skewton and Mrs. Gradgrind. That he didn't understand women is a modern truism that is no less applicable to other men of his time. That he didn't admit the claims of particular women that he knew, once he had turned against them, to any sort of intelligence, justification, or respect is a greater sign of Dickens's special idiosyncrasies of character. His relationships with men allowed gray areas and gradations of feeling. He had a falling-out with Douglas Jerrold but made friends again and exerted himself to benefit his wife and daughter; his friendship with Forster changed and he came to disapprove of several aspects of Forster's personality, but he never turned away from him completely. He did not always get along with Thackeray, and was quite possibly aware of the intermittent animus and envy Thackeray expressed toward him, but he either accorded him respect or kept quiet (until Thackeray took Catherine's part in Dickens's divorce). While he was frequently angry with and contemptuous of his father, he was reconciled to him toward the end of his father's life and treated him affectionately. But even Miss Coutts, his partner in charitable works, with whom he had what might be considered a more manly friendship, since it was based on common projects more than affectional feelings, never returned to a state of intimacy with him once he felt she betrayed him.

Dickens felt that he paid a price for the intensity of his imagination. In September, he wrote to Forster, "I am always deeply sensible of the wonderful exercise I have of life and its highest sensations, and I have said to myself for years, and have honestly and truly felt, this is a drawback to such a career [of writing novels] and is not to be complained of." But things had changed. He continued, "But the years have not made it easier to bear for either of us; and, for her sake as well as mine, the wish will force itself upon me that something might be done." A few days later, he wrote to Forster again, reconfirming his resolve to act by countering Forster's arguments, "She [Catherine] is exactly what you know, in the way of being amiable and complying; but we are strangely ill-assorted for the bond there is between us . . . and if I were sick or disabled tomorrow, I know how sorry she would be, and how deeply grieved myself, to think how we had lost each other. But exactly the same incompatibility would arise, the moment I was well again; and nothing on earth could make her understand me, or suit us to each other. Her temperament will not go with mine. It mattered not so much when we had only ourselves to consider, but reasons have been growing since which make it all but hopeless that we should even try to struggle on. What is now befalling me I have seen steadily coming, even since the days you remember when Mary was born. . . ." Mary was now nineteen years old.

What was happening to Dickens is all too recognizable to those of us living in the divorce culture—as long as he was committed to the marriage, the situation seemed endurable, if not desirable, but the appearance of an alternative retrospectively transformed not only his entire experience of the marriage, but his view of his wife's experience. There is actually no evidence at this point, or later, except what Dickens himself reported, that Catherine ceased to love Dickens or that she would not have chosen to remain in the marriage. Even Dickens admits that she continued "amiable and complying," but he steadily recasts their life together in order to justify its coming end. In October, he wrote to Forster, "Too late to say, put the curb on, and don't rush at hills—the wrong man to say it to."

Also in October, the Ternan family returned from Doncaster and took rooms in London. Ellen got an acting job at the Theatre Royal, Haymarket, and worked there for most of the next two years. Dickens seems to have been instrumental in getting her the job and wrote a note thanking the theater manager for the favor in mid-October. But if he expected immediate gratification in his new relationship, he seems to have been disappointed. He remained in a restless and anxious state of flux, unable to begin a new novel or to bring his family situation to closure. In fact, as his marriage moved toward open rupture and divorce, he encountered the most disagreeable side to his life as a public man; he was brewing up a scandal in which he was required to play the villain's role, and for at least the next year he played it, willy-nilly, to the hilt.

At the same time, he was moving toward giving public readings for money. Before Christmas, he gave two benefit readings of *A Christmas Carol*. In the late winter, he gave a fund-raising speech for the Hospital for Sick Children, which was still struggling to establish itself. The speech was so eloquent that it raised £3,000 (roughly comparable to $100,000 today) in one night. And Ackroyd reports an incident in which Dickens went with Forster to a playwright's reading of his own play and demonstrated afterward how the playwright should have read his own work. A bystander reported that, by contrast to the playwright's rendition, "the characters seemed to stand out and almost walk about the room." Queen Victoria let it be known that she wanted to hear *A Christmas Carol* at a private reading, but Dickens was reluctant, feeling that he needed an audience to create the best effect. Then he did another benefit reading in a large hall in Edinburgh, now consciously preparing himself and his material for his new moneymaking project. The reading was a tremendous success, confirming Dickens in his decision to go on with the idea, and in April he gave his first paid public reading. Many tickets were sold, the audience was receptive from the beginning, and Dickens asserted from the platform that his primary justification for what was considered by some to be an unorthodox and even undignified activity was that "whatever brings a public man and his public face to face, on terms of mutual confidence and respect, is a good thing." To his friends he confided two other motives—his unsettled personal life made him especially restless, and he wanted to make a lot of money in a short time.

Knowing as we do the great success of Dickens's new endeavor, and the great passion and talent that he brought to it, giving public performances of his work seems in retrospect to have been a natural flowering and integration of several of his signal talents. It is hard to understand quite what had been holding him back without remembering the social taint that surrounded both public performance and the appearance of working for money. Forster disapproved in part because he had gotten a little stuffy in the 1850s, but also because Dickens himself had worked over the years to make novel writing a respectable endeavor. Forster worried that the public readings would endanger Dickens's respectability and the respectability of the novel. But, in fact, Dickens was not respectable;

he had just finished attacking "respectability" in *Little Dorrit*, and he still did not fit into English middle-class life. He still acted on his deep-seated urge for freedom, although the consequences of doing so were often painful. He began to have new associates, younger and more like Wilkie Collins than Forster; some of his former associates, for example the middle-class Hogarths, whom he had once been pleased to join, he now detested. Thus it is instructive to look upon this juncture in Dickens's life in terms of its expression of his relationship to English class structure. He had realized his parents' ambition to be taken as stable members of the middle class and raised his own children to live in the middle class without any real alternative. But for himself he had reserved, with increasing difficulty and inner turmoil, the freedom to witness, criticize, and eventually break out of the middle class, at first through his art and then through his actions. The public readings were a gamble that could have more than a monetary payoff. When they worked as quality performances that were also popular and remunerative, they confirmed that Dickens was beyond class, that he was, as he called himself, "the Inimitable," a unique, entirely national treasure. Thus, again, he prefigures the modern period, where celebrities are required to throw off their allegiances to specific places or backgrounds and to exercise the freedom to be claimed by every paying customer. The professional Dickens, like the professional Rita Hayworth or the professional Paul Newman, inherently asserts the human kinship that goes beyond class. It is assumed that nuances of style or characterization or performance or insight can be comprehended by all members of the audience, whatever their class and educational background.

Dickens had asserted this before, in writing to be read aloud, in writing for monthly and weekly serials, in writing of the triumphs and tribulations of working-class characters, in criticizing English society and culture. But now, in taking up public readings and being exquisitely responsive to his audience (he always wanted them to laugh and cry openly, preferably in quick succession), he asserted it again and more strongly.

After the first reading in London, he continued to read systematically, in London for three months and then in the rest of England, Scotland, and Ireland for another three months. In the meantime, he and his friends were fashioning his divorce from Catherine. The catalyst for the open breach seems to have been Catherine's discovery that Dickens had given a piece of jewelry to Ellen Ternan, followed by jealousy, followed by some sort of demand on Dickens's part that Catherine visit or apologize to the Ternans. Possibly, having been found out enraged Dickens; he announced to Catherine that they would be separated (there is no record of the actual events, only several versions supplied by several sources). He proposed successive plans, ranging from the public appearance of harmony covering the actuality of separation through various forms of living apart, including the idea of Catherine moving, alone, to France, while Dickens and Georgina maintained the household and the children. Catherine, who had always been slow, compliant, and well-meaning, was no doubt appalled by what was happening to her and turned to her family, particularly her mother and younger sister. After that, the conflict became truly acrimonious, with accusations and rumors of an astounding nature, principally that Dickens had committed incest with Georgina and that Georgina was actually the mother of the Dickens children. Georgina was then examined by a doctor and discovered to be a virgin, at which point that particular accusation was dropped. From this, though, Dickens developed a sense of himself as the injured party that stuck with him for the rest of his life and fueled a strong hatred for the Hogarths and for almost everyone who took Catherine's side in the dispute. Even Miss Coutts was not, in the end, forgiven.

Dickens's bad behavior in the divorce extended to an attempt to alienate the children from their mother, which he justified by declaring that she had always been a bad mother and that the children, especially his daughters, did not care for her (which they later contradicted). One of them considered this behavior on their father's part "wicked," and the other considered it "mad," but no one could prevail on Dickens not to see it through, no matter what the implications or the consequences. Once he had identified himself as the Hogarths' victim, he proceeded to repudiate all relationships with anyone who had relationships with them. While the children were allowed to visit their mother, they were instructed to leave at once if Mrs. Hogarth or Catherine's sister happened to be there.

Not only did Dickens act out of fury, he also expressed his fury in public, though he disguised it as self-justification. On May 25, he wrote a letter to his readings manager, with a cover note asking him to show it around. The letter, which came to be known as the "violated" letter, asserted that the separation had long been Catherine's idea, because she was not suited to life with him; that she had never taken care of the children because of some "peculiarity of her character," but instead had them brought up by Georgina. Of Georgina, he also says, "Nothing has, on many occasions, stood between us and a separation but Mrs. Dickens' sister." He goes on to state that he is acting only in the interests of others, and that he and his children are in full agreement on every aspect of the conflict. Needless to say, others' accounts differed from Dickens's own, and the actions of such principals as Dickens's son Charley, now twenty-one, and Catherine herself did not fit in logically with Dickens's version. But once he had written it down, it became the truth for him, and he adhered to the idea that everything he did, including making Catherine a generous allowance, "as if Mrs. Dickens were a lady of distinction and I a man of fortune," had been misconstrued by enemies who unforgivably betrayed him.

Much of the letter is about the innocent purity of Georgina. In the last paragraph, he alludes to "the name of a young lady for whom I have a great attachment and regard." The beginning of the paragraph, a reference to "two wicked persons," who are probably Mrs. Hogarth and her youngest daughter, would indicate that he was referring to Georgina, but another incident shows that he was very sensitive to other rumors. Thackeray, going into a club where Dickens was also a member, was told that Dickens was sleeping with his sister-in-law, and he replied, "No, it's an actress." When his reply got back to Dickens, Dickens was enraged.

The letter, going about, did not have the justifying effect that Dickens had counted on, but rather fanned the rumors and the general disapproval. Dickens had not reckoned with the impossibility of proving a negative, and he had no press agent to muzzle him. He then went on to an even larger public mistake.

He decided that a public statement was necessary to counteract the rumors that were going about, so in early June he composed another letter, which he sent to various organs of the media and also published in *Household Words*. A hundred fifty years later, it is still an embarrassment to read, an aggressive floundering in the mire of public infamy that asserts that the situation is unimportant and not a problem for the participants, except for the "misrepresentations, most grossly false, most monstrous, and most cruel . . . and so widely spread that I doubt if one reader in a thousand will peruse these lines, by whom some touch of the breath of these slanders will not have passed, like unwholesome air." This letter did not have the desired effect either, mostly because far fewer readers than Dickens thought were privy to his troubles, so it caused rumors to proliferate rather than otherwise, as, of course, new speculations were added to old ones. Dickens wished the letter to appear in several publications, and many declined, most notably *Punch,* which was published by Bradbury and Evans, the publishers of *Household Words.* The *Punch* group included Thackeray and several others, with whom Dickens was never intimate again after his divorce.

In the course of legal negotiations concerning the settlement, which took place during May, trustees had to be appointed for both parties; and Frederick Evans, Dickens's publisher, was appointed as one trustee for Catherine, along with Dickens's friend and the editor of *Punch,* Mark Lemon. They apparently took up her cause with some reluctance.

Evans, in particular, became her protector (she later moved to a house not far from him). With absolutely no understanding that the situation required her trustees to negotiate for her in good faith, Dickens subsequently broke off relations with both of them, consigning them to the ranks of the unforgivable. Since one of them was his publisher, that meant that all of his publishing enterprises, including *Household Words,* had to be renegotiated. At first, Dickens tried to buy out the quarter interest in the magazine belonging to Bradbury and Evans, but they wouldn't sell, so Dickens announced in November that he was folding the magazine. In February 1859, he began work on another magazine of the same type, which he named *All the Year Round* and which he and his subeditor, W. H. Wills, owned 75 percent/25 percent and published themselves. As for his novels, he returned to Chapman and Hall for book publication. Edward Chapman, his old publisher, with whom he had broken when Chapman suggested that he pay back part of the advance for *Martin Chuzzlewit,* had since been bought out by a cousin, Frederic Chapman, who had a larger and more commercial business plan.

Dickens's divorce put all of his friends and acquaintances to the test. Indeed, it puts his biographers to the test, too. His actions throughout were hasty, self-serving, frequently furious, and often cruel. He showed a consistent inability to understand or sympathize with anyone who opposed his wishes or his views. Of his own accord, he foolishly carried his private concerns into the public arena, gratuitously damaging his reputation without, it seems, even realizing he was doing so. His biographer, like his friends, is required to somehow account for his behavior, especially since kindness and compassion had been two of his hallmark qualities throughout his career. His daughter later stated, "It brought out what was weakest in him," indicating that his behavior during the divorce was an extreme and prolonged variation of modes of behavior that were already part of his character. Peter Ackroyd makes a consistent case in his biography that Dickens was always prickly, always ready to see himself as a victim, and habitually tempted to blame others when things went wrong. The sources of these behaviors Ackroyd finds in Dickens's characteristic hypersensitivity (to everything, not just to slights and injuries), combined with the various shames and embarrassments of his childhood. As always, he felt things with desperate intensity. Because he had suppressed his feelings for a long time, once he began to reveal them, he also revealed the profound resentment that accompanied their long suppression, which in turn compelled ever more open revelation of them.

We also see a pattern in his behavior that is more familiar in our divorce culture than it was in Dickens's time—a man filled with conflicting passions, resentments, and needs transfers his allegiance from one object to another. The situation with the new woman requires him to suppress his demands or resentments with her in order to court her, so he displaces his anger onto the former object, changing entirely from the protective, considerate husband he had once been into a thoughtless tyrant, completely unable to dissemble, as he had been doing when the probable continuation of the marriage required it. More and more anger requires more and more self-justification, until the man literally comes to seem either "mad" or "wicked," which is what Dickens seemed to his daughters. At the same time, the man himself repeatedly talks about how forgetting the whole situation is the primary goal, as Dickens asserted in his public letter, in the lines "It [the situation] is amicably composed, and its details have now but to be forgotten by those concerned in it." But, of course, it was unlikely that anyone would soon forget it, and no one did. Catherine, though, maintained her loyalty to her husband for the rest of her life, going to productions of his work and keeping up with his publications. Ackroyd records no instances of anger or recrimination, either in public or in writing, on her part, but only a reluctant acceptance of the terms he proposed to her and a diminishing disruption of her relationship with her children as time went on (especially after Dickens's death). Charley, who was her designated protector, maintained good relations with Thackeray, Evans, and the others whom his father could not forgive, and he eventually married Evans's daughter against his father's wishes.

It is also true that the evidence of Dickens's vast canvas of characters, which includes Uriah Heep as well as David Copperfield, and Rigaud as well as Arthur Clennam, and Carker the manager and Joey Bagstock and the dwarf Quilp as well as John Jarndyce and Nicholas Nickleby and Sam Weller, indicates that Dickens was entirely at ease imagining anger, manipulation, and evil. Whatever the inspiration for any character, each receives life from the author's empathetic imagination, which is quickened through its sense of kinship with the idiosyncrasies of the character. Dickens's evil characters are often remarkable and riveting in their energy. They show that the powerful anger and longing Dickens expressed at the time of his divorce were not at all unknown or unfamiliar to him. Their eruption into his normally well-conducted life was possibly to be deplored, but also to be expected. Some of his contemporary authors were horrified at how he was behaving and did not themselves behave with a similar lack of control or degree of passion, but neither do their works explore the negative passions so deeply or so repeatedly. Once again, Dickens did not fit in and showed himself both freer and broader in his passions than those around him. But it is this very freedom and breadth that causes us to mention Dickens and not, say, Thackeray or Eliot, along with Shakespeare.

When she met Charles Dickens, Ellen Ternan was eighteen years old, neither as self-confident in her career nor as accomplished as her older sisters. Those biographers who have acknowledged Ellen Ternan's presence in Dickens's life (Forster did not, though Dickens wrote to him about his feelings almost from the beginning, and Forster reproduced Dickens's will, in which he left Ellen Ternan £1,000, as an appendix to the biography) have consistently wondered what qualities she had that he found so attractive that he was willing to throw his life into public turmoil for her sake. In addition to the treatment she has received in biographies of Dickens, she has been the subject of many rumors and at least one full-length biography of her own. She was important in his life from this point to its end, in 1870, but no one can say for sure whether she was his mistress, whether she bore any children by him, even whether she returned his affections. The most any biographer has been able to do is extrapolate from the female characters in his late novels and from his evident fondness for his sister Fanny, Mary Hogarth, and Georgina Hogarth (virginal figures) and his disenchantment with his wife and his mother (maternal figures). While the events are interesting, and would be even more so if we knew what they were, what is really interesting is how they brought out Dickens's secretiveness, something that was in part imposed upon him by both celebrity and the nature of Victorian society, where any taint upon a woman's reputation impaired her social position, but was also evident as a feature of his personality from the beginning, in the remoteness that alternated with his conviviality, in his love of disguise, in his solitary ramblings, in his attempts to send his parents out of the way to secluded spots, in the way in which he kept his early life to himself.

August 1857 marked a turning point in Dickens's life. Previously, he lived a professional life and a domestic life that were more or less open to scrutiny; his private reservations and ambivalences were displaced through activity, novel writing, and performance. After he met Ellen Ternan, he lived two lives, dividing his time and activities between what could be, and had to be, public, his working life, and what could not in any way be public, his affectional life. The man who had as large a role as anyone in creating "Victorian Englishness," that domestic ideal of comfort, coziness, business, and celebration, henceforth lived his life in direct contradiction to that very ideal. He was good at it. He made it so that his colleagues, his friends, his family, and his public were unaware of where and how he was spending at least some of his time. It was clear to everyone that his health and vitality were deteriorating almost from this point on, but everyone attributed the deterioration to the public readings he undertook and the energy he poured into them. He kept his secret life so well hidden that no biographer can gauge with any authority what he gained or lost by it, how he viewed it or justified it to himself, how his feelings for Ellen Ternan evolved, whether she satisfied those yearnings for true intimacy that he had expressed to Forster and found unsatisfied in his wife, whether he found at least intermittent peace with Ellen or only continuing frustration. There is no telling what she was like. An acquaintance wrote some years later that as an older woman, she was "witty, warm, sympathetic, charming, cultured, and charitable," that she "victimized" her husband and "made scenes," and she was teasing, self-willed, and a "spitfire." But there is no way of knowing which of these qualities, if any, were original, and attracted Dickens to her, and which were, perhaps, reactions to her relationship with a man almost thirty years her senior whose behavior toward her remains unknown.

The modern era of divorce has shown that individuals' modes of behavior in relationships sometimes change in interesting ways, depending upon what the person learns about himself or herself from previous relationships. Usually the man or woman is helped to these lessons by therapists or sympathetic friends or even books. The bête noire of modern life is "making the same mistakes over again" or, indeed, over and over again. If we speculate that, once again prefiguring modern life, Dickens entered into a remarriage of a sort without the benefit of the divorce culture that guides such things today, and that he "made the same mistakes over again," then most likely his behavior continued to be of a piece, and he was with Ellen as he had been with the other women in his life—domineering, exacting, prickly, and sensitive to slights, but also kind, affectionate, generous, and lively, as well as sexually passionate, though the mystery of whether Ellen Ternan ever bore his child reflects the mystery of whether the two ever became lovers. After ten children, many of whom were becoming troublesome as they neared adulthood, it is possible that Dickens decided that abstinence was the wiser course. Dickens succeeded in his secretiveness as he did in almost all of his endeavors, but the deterioration of his health showed that the price of the contradictions he had to live with was a high one. At the very least, he now had one more reason to travel constantly, to have several homes and sometimes even rooms that he rented, none of which could hold him for very long.

After 1859, for the next eleven years, Dickens lived so secret a life that Ellen Ternan's place in it did not emerge at all until 1934. The figure his family, friends, and audiences saw was of a man frantically using up his energy and his health giving strenuous and emotionally taxing public readings while editing a weekly periodical and writing three major novels—*A Tale of Two Cities, Great Expectations,* and *Our Mutual Friend.* Commentators have seen Ellen in the angelic figure of Lucie Manette, in the unattainable figure of Estella, in the playful, money-hungry figure of Bella Wilfer. It is, of course, always tempting to extrapolate from an author's work to his state of mind, and Dickens did have a history of explicitly depicting associates in his work—Leigh Hunt in *Bleak House,* Georgina Hogarth in *Bleak House,* Maria Beadnell Winter in *Little Dorrit.* But each time he communicated to someone, usually Forster, what he was doing and how he was modifying the original to make him or her, supposedly, less recognizable. Dickens's daughter maintained after his death that he didn't understand women, but, in fact, the portraits of women in his last three completed novels are more complex and interesting than in earlier novels. Miss Pross, in *A Tale of Two Cities,* for example, is explicitly declared to have more than one layer: "Mr. Lorry knew Miss Pross to be very jealous, but he also knew her by this time to be, beneath the surface of her eccentricity, one of those unselfish creatures—found only among women—who will, for pure love and admiration, bind themselves willing slaves, to youth when they have lost it, to beauty that they never had, to accomplishments that they were never fortunate enough to gain, to bright hopes that never shone upon their own sombre lives." Rather than starting out with a Flora Finching, who *is* her main characteristic at the beginning and gradually develops depth, he defines Miss Pross immediately, in the voice of the narrator, as complex. Unlike Flora and Miss Tox, she doesn't have to earn her way out of being ridiculous (and physically unappealing women are often portrayed as ridiculous in Dickens's works). The evidence, though slim, is that Dickens learned something about women from the crucible of his divorce and showed it in his work almost immediately.

In 1837, when Dickens himself was a young man and just married, Thomas Carlyle published *History of the French Revolution.* Dickens said later that he carried it everywhere with him, and he read it many times over the years. After 1840, when Dickens met Carlyle and his wife, Jane, at a party, they formed a friendship that was marked by reverence on Dickens's part. (He told Forster, "I would go . . . farther to see

Carlyle than any man alive.") Carlyle's feelings were more mixed, partly because he did not respect novels or novelists (though his writing style and historiographic style were far more novelistic than would be considered objective or professional today). At any rate, by 1858, when Dickens began to think about *A Tale of Two Cities,* he was eminently familiar with Carlyle's *History* and his interpretation of the important features of the French Revolution. By this time, also, Dickens had been to France so often and with such pleasure that he considered himself more than a Francophile, almost a Frenchman in exile. He spoke fluent French and had, in fact, through Mr. Meagles in *Little Dorrit* lampooned Englishmen who insisted upon making themselves understood abroad only by raising their voices. He would later expand his satire on narrow-minded Englishness in the figure of Podsnap in *Our Mutual Friend.*

A Tale of Two Cities was planned for the launch of *All the Year Round,* and Dickens seems to have begun writing in earnest in March, for publication at the end of April. Thereafter, the novel appeared in weekly installments until November. Commercially, it was a huge success. The first issue sold 120,000 copies (though, of course, some portion of the sale must have been due to the novelty appeal of the new magazine) and then settled down to about 100,000 copies. Sales of monthly parts were not as good, but in volume form it has always since been the steady bestseller of Dickens's oeuvre.

Dickens planned to try a few new things with the novel, and whether they succeeded or not in the view of friends and critics, he did produce a novel that is in some ways not as "Dickensy" as his other works. He had a stronger grasp of the requirements (and perhaps the impossibilities) of the historical novel than he had had with *Barnaby Rudge,* and he was able to consciously subdue some of his own habits of imagination in order to represent as truly as possible the nonrepresentable—that is, a historical period that the author had not personally experienced.

The paradox of the historical novel is that it purports to give life and spirit to the past in a way that historical accounts themselves, with their emphasis on interpretation and fidelity to facts, cannot. Of course, some historical periods are extremely dramatic, and imaginatively entering into them is quite tempting. In addition, an author like Dickens, who was interested in the workings of large social systems, is always curious about how the present system came to be, and so has a natural interest in history. And when the novel is first published, it may seem to be a true and faithful rendering of the life of the time it is looking back to, but almost every historical novel dates very quickly and soon comes to epitomize its own period more than the period in which it is set. A historical novel can be compromised by the simplest discovery of new material, but even if nothing new turns up, the style that the author has chosen to mimic the earlier period may no longer seem to do so. For all the research that goes into it, and for all the weight it seems to have, the historical novel is one of the most ephemeral genres and reveals most clearly an author's intellectual and imaginative limitations.

When Dickens sat down to research the novel, the Carlyles had an enormous box of books sent to him from the London Library. He intended not to contradict Carlyle's interpretation, but to give it the life of a dramatic tale. The period of the French Revolution was less than a hundred years in the past, as retrievable for him as World War I would be for us, the era of his grandparents. Forster later said, and the evidence of Dickens's letters supports the idea, that Dickens wanted the incidents, the history, and the plot to drive the characters, rather than his usual fashion of having the plot grow out of the characters and their situations. Specifically, he wanted them to develop through action rather than through dialogue. The novel did what Dickens intended—the characters do seem either dimmer or more normal, depending on the reader's taste. Forster didn't like the novel, and Dickens did have to defend it from time to time, but Dickens liked it and said, as he often did, that he thought it was the best thing he had written. It has not been as popular with scholars and critics as it has with readers, but there is a lot to be said for it.

For one thing, it is an exciting novel. Unlike the plot of *Little Dorrit,* that of *A Tale of Two Cities* is tight and clear, almost fairy tale–like. Dickens seems to have conceived of Sidney Carton and Dr. Manette first, intrigued by the idea of self-sacrifice, as with *The Frozen Deep,* and also with the idea of prolonged imprisonment. To our eyes, the tightness of the plot seems not very literary—a little Hollywood—and indeed, a couple of famous movies of *A Tale of Two Cities* were made. But the fact that everyone is related to everyone else, aside from reiterating Dickens's perennial theme of relationship, also pointedly asserts the moral complexity of political injury and revenge.

Dickens never goes easy on the pre-Revolutionary French aristocracy. As a group (represented by "Monseigneur," who requires four men to prepare and serve his chocolate), they are presented as repressive and cruel, locked in a world of unreality that they have created for themselves. Two nobles rape the daughter of a tenant, murder her brother, commit manslaughter of a child, impoverish and starve their tenants, and promote fear and intimidation as the proper mode of rule. If the sections of the novel about life in pre-Revolutionary France were excerpted and strung together, they would read like a call to revolution. Dickens shows that he perfectly understands what daily shapes the rage and zeal of the republicans—their undying hatred for their former rulers is the inevitable and perfect crop that the rulers themselves have sown.

In the context of this large historical movement, there seems to be some, though not much, room for personal choice. Hero Charles Darnay chooses not to profit from the exploitation of the peasantry and to work for an honest living in England, but he is sensitive to the moral confusion of his position when he hears from the family's former agent in prison: "He knew very well, that in his love for Lucie, his renunciation of his social place . . . had been hurried and incomplete. He knew that he ought to have systematically worked it out and supervised it, and that he had meant to do it, and that it had never been done." In addition, he is tempted. He is curious. He wonders if he might still have some influence for good. The Revolution has become for him, as Dickens calls it, "the Loadstone [*sic*] Rock"—"Everything that arose in his mind drifted him on, faster and faster, more and more steadily, to the terrible attraction." This is a masterstroke of motivation, finessing the improbability of Darnay's return to France as well as revealing Dickens's own recent experience of the psychological process of giving in to the temptation of change and chaos. The plot turns on Darnay's unlikely choice, and it is utterly convincing.

In fact, a major theme of the book is this very temptation—the temptation of the unknown, especially when it is embodied in violent action. To give in to the temptation, as the republicans do when they dance the carmagnole, as the Evremonde brothers do when they rape and murder, as Madame Defarge does when she sets out to find Lucie and her child in order to denounce them, is to set in motion one's own destruction. The novel urges a proto-Freudian analysis of human nature—the harshness and unreality of the superego is finally overthrown by the id, unleashing a vast, destructive, natural force (the mobs are often represented by images of fire and flood), leaving no rational middle ground for the operation of the ego, which is defined by moral connections of right and wrong, responsibility and choice among individuals. The horrors committed by the id—that is, the republicans—do not have quite the same moral perversity of those committed by the superego, because the ego (reason) has not been falsely enlisted to justify inhumanity. The republicans know they are killing other people, but the nobles consider the peasants to be animals. The republicans know, as well, that they are numbed by death. In one interesting passage, Lucie appeals to Madame Defarge for mercy, "as a wife and mother." Madame Defarge responds, " 'All our lives, we have seen our sister-women suffer, in themselves and in their children, poverty, nakedness, hunger, thirst, sickness, misery, oppression and neglect of all kinds.'

" 'We have seen nothing else,' returned The Vengeance [Madame Defarge's friend].

" 'We have borne this a long time,' said Madame Defarge. 'Judge you! Is it likely that the trouble of one wife and mother would be much to us now?' "

Like the characters of *Little Dorrit,* those of *A Tale of Two Cities* are trapped by the past. Revolution offers an interesting collective answer—destroy the institutions and relationships and citizens and thought patterns of the past. In this sense, the Terror is Dickens's next step after the final image of the earlier novel. Rather than allowing individuals to be swallowed up in the "usual uproar," clear away the usual uproar and see what happens. But the outcome is even worse—the usual uproar gives way to an unusual and far more destructive uproar.

Only Sydney Carton elects not to be trapped by his past, and the solution Dickens gives him is specific—he understands that his physical life is of no importance compared with his spiritual life. When he changes places with Darnay and goes to his execution, he is connected to another human being (the little seamstress whom he comforts) and fully aware that his being will continue in the memories and relationships of those who love him. More important, at the very moment of Carton's death, Dickens writes, "I am the Resurrection and the Life, saith the Lord: he that believeth in me, though he were dead, yet shall he live: and whosoever liveth in me shall never die." In a world where the superego, the id, and the ego have all failed, only the spirit succeeds. Carton asserts several times that he doesn't feel his death to be a sacrifice. Modern critics have taken issue with him, but Dickens asserts as strongly as he can at the end that the death of the body can and should be seen as a transfiguration, not as a sacrifice or a capitulation.

Dickens's religious beliefs are often the subject of debate, partly because he ridiculed Evangelicalism relentlessly, in figures like Dr. Chadband in *Bleak House* and Mrs. Clennam in *Little Dorrit,* but he was never backward in offering an alternative faith. For him the figure of Jesus Christ was a consistent image of salvation. Love, kindness, forgiveness, benevolence, celebration, mercy, joy, charity, and innocence all had their source, for Dickens, in Christ and Christmas. That these concepts had been crusted over by organized religion, not only Evangelicalism, but the corrupt and unresponsive religion of the Church of England and of the Catholic Church, did not mean that they had no existence or reality, only that their existence and reality were available solely within and among individuals.

Of course, it is not surprising that, given the recent chaos of his life and the violence of his feelings, Dickens should choose the most violent possible subject matter for his novel and that he should depict it with vivid relish. Authors often choose subjects that are analogues to their states of mind and extrapolate successfully from individual turmoil to social or even universal turmoil. Seeing these analogues and making them understandable and believable is one of a novelist's social roles. What is especially interesting about Dickens is that he unerringly engaged with almost every aspect of modern culture, hardly missing a single one. To read *A Tale of Two Cities* after the close of the violent and ideological twentieth century is to be struck over and over by the prophetic nature of his insights—the inability of the new regime to draw a line before "extermination," as Madame Defarge puts it; the inability of the old regime to understand what it has done wrong; the submersion of the individual into the collective; the suspiciousness of the collective toward any individual, no matter how respectable his "revolutionary credentials," who expresses doubt (as Defarge does); the elevation of ideology over relationship; the destruction of love (as between the Defarges); the moral tangle of denunciation. Dickens himself said that he did not add new insights to those of Carlyle, but he clearly and systematically made them live through character and plot, and in the process included revolution as yet another aspect of his analysis of modernity.

Every novel is a chance for the author to get at the insoluble conundrum of the novel in a new way. It is no coincidence that the disordered and tortured plot of *Little Dorrit* (which requires an explanation at the end to make the connections clear) was followed by the clear and compelling plot of *A Tale of Two Cities*. It is also no coincidence that the earlier novel is held in greater esteem by critics, while the later novel is more popular. The primacy of action in the latter work produces suspense; the primacy of character in the former work produces contemplation and analysis. But *A Tale of Two Cities* is no less wise than the previous novel, no less insightful, no less bleak, for that matter, since it doesn't even make an effort to resolve the conflict between the superego and the id, except through death, redemption, and the passage of time.

Dickens wrote most of *A Tale of Two Cities* at Gad's Hill Place, where he lived with Georgina and the children. His old convivial life was more or less behind him now. He no longer spoke to some of his former companions, and he was both depressed and unwell. A Boston publisher came to visit and tried to persuade Dickens to undertake an American reading tour. Dickens was agreeable; negotiations with various impresarios continued into the next year, but the Civil War broke out before anything certain could be arranged. Meanwhile, in October, he toured the provinces, as always with a huge response from his audiences—weeping, laughter, applause. Undeniably, his life was more orderly now, and he managed his restlessness somewhat better, with long country walks. He worked on *All the Year Round,* sent another letter to George Eliot, and went to dinner with her and G. H. Lewes, who lived together unmarried (although he addressed her as "Mrs. Lewes" anyway). He invited her to write for his magazine. She was unable to find the time. He made speeches for various charitable organizations. He went about fourteen months between the end of *A Tale of Two Cities* and the beginning of *Great Expectations* without writing another novel, but he did begin a series of pieces in *All the Year Round* that were later collected in *The Uncommercial Traveller.*

In July, his second daughter, Katey, married Wilkie Collins's brother, Charles. Katey was twenty, a vivacious girl anxious to leave home. She had loved one of Dickens's friends, but he was unresponsive, so she married Collins, she said later, just to get away from "an unhappy home." To all appearances, the July 17 wedding was a bright, celebratory occasion, but when Mamie, the older daughter, went up to Katey's room at the end of the day, she "beheld her father on his knees with his head buried in Katey's wedding gown, sobbing." He said, "But for me, Katey would not have left home." Dickens's children were all in their teens and early twenties at the time of the divorce. It is safe to say that of the

nine living children, only one, Henry, made a successful career. All the rest of the boys were irresponsible and profligate
with money, like Dickens's father and two of his brothers.
Mamie never married, and Kate's marriage was not a happy
one. Dickens himself found his sons' inability to settle on
their careers or to get ahead unaccountable, evidence not of
his failure as a parent but of something wrong in them. He
compared their fecklessness with his own youthful ambition
and energy and found them wanting. His novels abound with
feckless young men—James Harthouse in *Hard Times,* for example, and, in *Our Mutual Friend,* Mortimer Lightwood and
Eugene Wrayburn, whose easy manners are so galling to the
ambitious, Dickens-like characters Bradley Headstone and
Charlie Hexam. Once again, the plight of his children seems
more understandable to us than it did to him: a bad marriage;
a bitter divorce during their most vulnerable years; a secretive,
demanding, capricious father, who was apart from them
much of the time, who moved them frequently from place to
place, and who was himself changeable—often charming and
attentive, but also often remote and angry; a caretaker
(Georgina) who, whatever her good qualities, was not much
older than the older children when she took over their care;
the stresses of their father's extreme celebrity. It is hard not to
read into some of the disorganized large families he depicts,
such as the Pockets in *Great Expectations* or the Jellybys in
Bleak House, some aspects of his own household. Even
though in these depictions he puts all the blame upon the
mothers, we might say that the family system of the Dickens
household was not one in which the children were likely to
thrive, and they didn't.

CHAPTER SIX

JUST AFTER Katey's marriage, Dickens's brother Alfred died, and Dickens brought his family to London (there were five children). He sold Tavistock House and gave most of the furniture to his sister, who was taking care of his mother, who seems to have been a victim of some form of senile dementia. From then on, Gad's Hill Place was his home, though he also spent some time, at least, in rooms he rented and at a house he bought for Ellen Ternan in Houghton Place, in London (she sold the lease on the house in 1881). At the beginning of October 1860, he began work on *Great Expectations*.

Dickens had been thinking of ideas and seems to have first come up with the notion of Pip and Magwitch, his fairy godfather/convict, thinking the idea a funny one and a return to an old comic style. His first plan was to write a novel of the length and form of *Little Dorrit*—twenty monthly parts. He had found the weekly schedule of *A Tale of Two Cities* very exhausting and the format constricting. But the serial running in *All the Year Round* was driving down profits and circulation, even to the point of threatening the solvency of the magazine, so almost as soon as he began writing, he started publishing the novel to perk things up. In spite of bouts of depression and ill health, in spite of his griefs and frustrations, his inventive energy did not fail him. The thirty-six installments of the novel were completed without much trouble, and Dickens, as always, was pleased with them.

While Forster and others approved Dickens's return to a more comic style, it is hard in some ways to see what they were talking about. The novel opens with Pip standing in the graveyard of the small village in the Kentish marshes where his parents and brothers are buried. Everyone around the boy (who seems to be about eight or nine) is either cruel or foolish, including Joe Gargery, his kindly brother-in-law, who is unable to protect Pip (or himself) from the unreasoning abusive treatment meted out by Pip's sister. The glow of early acceptance and love present in *David Copperfield,* before it is poisoned by the Murdstones, is entirely absent in *Great Expectations,* and Pip's world offers no alternative to harsh discipline and ridicule. When Pip's companionship is solicited by Miss Havisham for some mysterious reason of her own, the world she and Estella inhabit is even stranger than the world of the village, and Miss Havisham is no less ready to abuse and ridicule Pip than his sister is. The loving companionship of Joe is less than effective in easing Pip's condition, since any hint of collaboration between the two is met by the sister with even more resentment. These three women, plus Mrs. Pocket (entirely irresponsible and self-important) and Miss Havisham's female relatives (parasites who hope only to get a piece of her estate upon her death), are hardly offset in their female monstrousness by Biddy, a girl of the village who seems to love Pip but is just another, and rather less well realized, of Dickens's Esther Summerson types.

In addition, Pip is constantly beset by doubts about his own intentions and nature. Whereas David knows the injustices of the world for what they are, Pip has a strong sense of guilt, which renders his response to obvious injustices more ambivalent. He holds himself accountable (and Dickens seems to agree with him) for ignorance that to the reader he certainly cannot help. When Magwitch, in the first chapter, threatens him in order to get him to steal food from his sister's larder, Pip goes on at some length about his sense of guilt at this, contradicting the reader's feeling that surely a nine-year-old boy is not to be blamed for being coerced by a frightening escaped criminal. This is not to say that Pip's psychology is unbelievable, only that it is not exactly comic. Comedy requires belief in innocence. Pip never believes in his own innocence, and much of the rhetoric of the novel is geared toward convincing the reader that Pip is *not* innocent—he might not be especially blameworthy at the beginning, but as he gets older and rises in his expectations, his sins of profligacy, ingratitude, and fecklessness become real. David Copperfield, by contrast, has much to learn, and his arc through the novel is the arc of his moral education—his flaw is to attach himself to morally flawed characters like Steerforth and to blind himself to their faults. Pip's flaw is to have no discrimination at all, but to withhold himself from everyone, unsure at all times what value they have for him and what value he has for them. Once again, a portrait full of psychological truth, but far from comic. And Dickens knows this instinctively—although Pip is morally redeemed by the end, he cannot get all the way to satisfaction or happiness. Neither the original ending, where he and Estella meet and part, nor the second ending, recommended by Forster, where they meet with a hint that they do not part, but with no depiction of their life together, is in any way a comic ending. Of all the heroes of Dickens's fiction, Pip is the only one too flawed, by self-hatred and shame, to find no reward other than mere survival. Like Louisa in *Hard Times,* Pip finds domestic satisfaction in witnessing the satisfaction of others—Joe and Biddy, Herbert and Clara. The redemptions of Miss Havisham and Magwitch do not benefit Pip, nor do they entirely lift the burden of guilt from the novel. Pip's sense of himself as undeserving grows more sophisticated, but it remains. Dickens presses Pip's sense of his own guilt a little too hard, and in this the moral argument of the novel seems slightly off.

In the version of *Great Expectations* we have, we can see the ghost of the version Dickens originally planned—more on the scale of *Little Dorrit* than *A Tale of Two Cities.* Shrinking his execution to fit the circumstances of *All the Year Round* streamlined the book but leaves fascinating themes and characters relatively unexplored. *Great Expectations* was a commercial and, with a couple of exceptions, a critical success. Forster liked it very much, and modern critics have adored it. It is totally Dickensy, yet shorter than the real Dickensy novels. Its shortness amounts to restraint. Its undeniable darkness is edged with light, in a kind of reverse of Dickens's youthful work, where the lightness was edged with black. Angus Wilson maintains that it is the one novel of his oeuvre wherein Dickens meets the criteria set by Flaubert and James for the well-made novel, and is therefore more perfect (though not greater) than his others. This is an interesting argument, because it suggests that novelistic greatness lies in the author's success in working out his vision most completely in his most characteristic manner. Dickens's manner, then, would be naturally unrestrained, so "perfection" would be less characteristic of him than vastness and variety; therefore his most perfect novel would be less characteristic and therefore less great than his more imperfect novels.

After the completion of *Great Expectations* in June 1861, Dickens seems to have embarked upon a double life that was marked by increasing ill health, mysterious disappearances, successful and remunerative reading tours, and the deaths of friends and relatives. In October of that year, his tour manager died, as well as his brother-in-law. His mother died, at the age of seventy-four, in 1863. Her death was followed by that of his son Walter (in India), only twenty-two years old, and that of Thackeray, in December (Thackeray was younger than Dickens). The next year, another old friend died, and in 1866, Jane Carlyle, and Dickens's brother Augustus, who had gotten as far as Chicago. In 1867, another old friend, Clarkson Stanfield, died in April, and in 1868, his brother Fred. In 1870, Daniel Maclise, the painter, died in the spring.

Other friends were thriving, though—notably the actor Charles Macready, who married a second wife thirty years his junior in 1861 and had a son with her at the age of sixty-eight, in 1862. Macready's remarriage reminds us that Dickens's choice to live two lives, one public and one secret, was, in spite of our conventional image of Victorian life, more in his own nature than in the social requirements of the time. Several of his friends, including Daniel Maclise and Wilkie Collins, as well as George Eliot and G. H. Lewes, managed to live openly in an irregular manner and were not especially ostracized for doing so. Given Dickens's open attacks on "Society" in *Dombey and Son* and all subsequent novels, and his penchant for rewarding his heroes and heroines with retired lives of honest labor and benevolence, rather than wealth and social position, his own resistance to the option of claiming Ellen Ternan as his mistress and making a life with her requires at least some investigation and explanation—one would think that social ostracism would be right up his alley. But he pursued secrecy with inveterate energy.

Almost no biographer has a good explanation for this, but Claire Tomalin, the author of a life of Ellen Ternan, speculates that vehement early assertions that his relations with Ellen were platonic and fatherly, and therefore that she was a virtuous young woman, like a daughter to him, gave him both a cover story and further motivation for secrecy. We already know from letters of 1858 that he created a version of his marriage that suited him—groundless jealousy on the part of Catherine, perfect virtue on the part of himself, Georgina, and the Ternans. Tomalin quotes a letter Dickens wrote to one of the Ternans' cousins, in which he protests the perfect innocence of his liaison with the family, yet the style and the circumstances of the letter indicate an unusual degree of intimacy. Mrs. Ternan is known to have made a reputation for herself and her daughters in the theatrical world that was based on both artistic and personal respectability—the progress of her career demonstrates the transitional but still questionable social status of acting, and particularly of actresses, through the nineteenth century. While all actresses were no longer considered automatically to be prostitutes, as they had been, their social status continued to be tainted by the display of themselves and their talents for money.

As time went on and Dickens's relationship with Ellen Ternan evolved (at one point, he provided the funds for Ellen's older sister to travel to Italy and study singing, chaperoned by her mother, leaving Ellen and her other sister unchaperoned in London), the habit of secrecy and the necessity of secrecy became inextricably entangled. Undoubtedly, the embarrassment he felt at the exposure of his family life during the months he was divorcing Catherine motivated him never to allow any sort of exposure again. Ackroyd makes the point that the worst part of Dickens's employment in the blacking factory was having to stand in the window and paste labels while passersby watched him. He made a contest of it and became marvelously quick, but perhaps this was a pattern in his behavior—if he was required to reveal himself, then he would do so as a phenomenon, but his real preference was for privacy. By the time he was in his fifties, as often happens, contradictory elements in his personality had become almost irreconcilably extreme. He was used to, and enjoyed, being a phenomenon and a star, and he courted unprecedented stardom in every aspect of his public readings, from the material he chose to the dramatic manner in which he rendered it. But the yearning for concealment was no less strong, so he made romantic arrangements that required concealment and possibly gained preciousness from that very concealment. Orthodox family life, with a large household, one child after another, and marriage had been a failure. A hidden affair—"a circle of one," as Dickens called it to one correspondent—possibly retained more piquancy and drama. And, at the very least, leading a double life gave Dickens's lifelong restlessness a point. He was now on the train all the time, traveling all the time, moving from Gad's Hill, to his bachelor flat above the offices of *All the Year Round* on Wellington Street, to the house in Houghton Place where Ellen lived, and later to the house in Slough, and later to the house in Peckham. It is also likely that Ellen and her mother lived for a couple of years in France, which would have been no problem for Dickens—rather an added pleasure, since he loved France and wrote more than once of his pleasure in setting out for French destinations.

Who was the audience for Dickens's secret life? Undoubtedly himself. He had a strong need to feel himself virtuous, youthful, benevolent, and important at all times. The friends he broke off with after the divorce were precisely those whom Dickens had betrayed himself in front of. Thackeray remarked that he could see through Dickens now. The others, like Mark Lemon and Miss Coutts, did not have to actually challenge him in order for him to feel that what they had seen of him and the way in which they reflected him back to himself was intolerable. They had gained knowledge of a side of him that he himself did not want to know, so he broke off relations. As with later public men and celebrities, his importance and power had led him to believe that he could do as he wished until he discovered that fame in the larger world is at least as constricting as, say, small-town notoriety.

Dickens and his work had always been contradictory. He professed virtue, and acted virtuously in the world, but he was drawn to crime, criminals, prostitutes, detectives, social disruption, and the Victorian underworld of hypocrisy, cruelty, ignorance, sickness, and death. Every novel he wrote explored innocence, but his innocent characters are far less alive than the villains, ne'er-do-wells, social climbers, usurers, cheats, liars, fools, murderers, grotesques, and madmen who surround them.

Once again, as with Mary Hogarth and Catherine, then with Catherine and Georgina, Dickens tried to strike a balance between his contradictory desires (which he felt with desperate intensity), this time between the public life of the readings and the secret life of his heart. We may suppose that his secret life was at least occasionally frustrating or unsatisfying, or even painful and tragic, and that at least some of the energy that went into his readings came from the secrets that he kept about his other life, as when, in the character of Richard Wardour in *The Frozen Deep,* he was able to express feelings that he could not reveal in person in a manner that almost overwhelmed his audience. Dickens may have felt, in fact, that the way he had structured his life—compartmentalizing it into several rather distant locations, one the family location, one the love location, one the *All the Year Round* location, one the fame location, with occasional holiday locations—worked wonderfully well to externalize his inner compartmentalization. In each location he had a faithful companion—Georgina, Ellen Ternan, W. H. Wills, and, for the readings, George Dolby, who was happy to assist and care for him—but they didn't have to get along with one another particularly often. Since he lived this way for thirteen years, the system must have worked well enough most of the time, but it was a taxing and delicate one and visibly told on his health (though one observer wrote in the summer of 1864, "I met Dickens . . . clad in spruce frockcoat, buttoned to show his good and still youthful figure; and with a brand-new hat airily cocked on one side, and stick poised in his hand").

Of all the things that a novelist does, the first among them is to make repeated attempts to rationalize the world. Every time he or she writes a novel, he or she is systematizing what seems chaotic to others. In order for the product to satisfy the novelist, it has to have a certain rightness about it; order of some kind, comprehensibility of some kind, and truth of some kind are always present. As the novelist masters his or her materials and techniques, his or her novels approach more and more closely the novelist's natural cast of mind, or most essential vision, and the logical or systematic qualities of the novel speak back to the novelist, confirming his or her power to make something real. It is thus a tremendous temptation for a novelist, especially a successful one, to attempt to transform the world itself so that it fits the novelist's sense of the right sort of life. Dickens was always both active and energetic in his attempts to make the world fit his model; education, charitable works, social criticism and activism, aid to friends and their families, essays and articles and novels—all attest to his will to shape the world to a certain idea, as does his insistence on quiet, order, good dress, and excellent behavior on the part of his children. Certainly much of Dickens's discomfort in his domestic life in the 1850s was due to an abiding feeling of wrongness—the wife and the children and the houses simply did not mesh, however strenuous his efforts, with what felt right, and vast expenditures of energy in changing this or that part of the picture had no effect. That the life that did finally mesh with his sense of rightness was unusual, marked by less and less resistance or opposition on the part of his associates, with its terms dictated by him, shouldn't surprise us, but neither should it surprise us that it was a life he could not easily live. A novelist's late, eccentric life is analogous to his late, eccentric novels. His ties to the mainstream have loosened. His primary job is no longer to be representative, as when he was a young writer looking for a publisher and an audience; it is to be still interesting. But it may be that those to whom he is still interesting are not his contemporaries, whose world he reflects, but his descendants, whose world he intuits and predicts. Long association has convinced his contemporaries that they know him; this will not necessarily be so for those who have a different historical perspective. As with the work, so with the life. In the last years of Dickens's life, he seems to have embraced a freer, more individualistic pattern, no longer striving to fit in, but actively seeking the sorts of relationships that are primary in our century—one-to-one intimacies on the one hand, joined with star-to-audience performances on the other. The intermediate circle of family, friends, clubs, and associations that had been a prominent feature of his thirties and forties had largely dropped away.

Dickens's reading tour in 1861 took him to twenty and more cities in two and a half months. He had earned £500 for six readings in the summer, so the work was profitable—the duration of the tour was short in comparison with the longer task of writing even one of his shorter novels (thirty to thirty-six weekly installments), not to mention a longer one (twenty installments over nineteen months). But Dickens was never one to stint on preparation. He rewrote, edited, and rehearsed each selection and came to feel that two hundred rehearsals was the minimum before the introduction of new material. His technique was not quite acting, but far more than reading aloud. He was especially good at modulating the nuances of every sentence, narrative as well as dialogue, in order to bring out its proper effect. Not a word was wasted—words and phrases and sentences that did well enough on the page were changed if they were a little flat in performance. His stage set was simple—a desk, a lamp, a few decorations. He strove to give the feeling of intimacy in even the largest halls and was a master at developing a sense of individual communication between himself and members of the audience, in part by not maintaining an impassive distance from them, but by reacting to what he was reading as they did. The original inspirations of his public readings were private readings of the Christmas books to groups of friends, and he saw no reason to change a successful model. Ellen Ternan and other friends were often in the audience. As his health declined, they could judge whether the readings were too strenuous, but he didn't always follow their advice. The winter reading series concluded at the end of January 1862.

English literary life was now full and varied. George Eliot followed *Scenes of Clerical Life* and *Adam Bede* with *The Mill on the Floss* (1860) and *Silas Marner* (1861). Tennyson published *Idylls of the King* (1859); George Meredith, *The Ordeal of Richard Feverel* (1859); Wilkie Collins, *The Woman in White* (1860). Samuel Smiles, J. S. Mill, Charles Darwin, Herbert Spencer, and John Ruskin were all active, in these years publishing their most famous works. In Russia, Turgenev was publishing *Fathers and Sons,* Dostoevsky was publishing *Notes from Underground,* and Tolstoy was at work on *War and Peace,* to be published in 1865. In France, Victor Hugo was publishing *Les Misérables,* Flaubert was publishing

Salammbô. Dickens was not much older than most of these writers (and younger than Mill and Darwin), but he was their ancestor as well as their contemporary. The thread of English fiction that led back to Scott came directly through Dickens. In his essay "Epic and Novel," the Russian literary theorist M. M. Bakhtin points out that of all the literary genres, only the novel does not predate Aristotle, and only the novel is not defined by Aristotelian poetics: "The novel is not merely one genre among other genres. Among genres already completed and in part already dead, the novel is the only developing genre. It is the only genre that was born and nourished in a new era of world history and therefore, it is deeply akin to that era." A genre doesn't develop of itself, of course. It develops because its practitioners have ideas and talents that enlarge the form to encompass phenomena that are new or have not been portrayed successfully before. If we take Jane Austen, for example, it is often observed that the servant classes, the colonial plantations, and the naval establishment that supported the lives of her characters are never alluded to or depicted in her novels. The reasons for this are no doubt a combination of habits of mind, considerations of artistic form, and convention, but the basic fact is that Austen didn't consider it necessary to broaden her canvas or her language. Dickens, about a generation younger than Austen and a descendant on his mother's side of one of those serving families who do not appear in any of Austen's work, found a way to satisfy his own urgent need to depict almost everyone in his English world who did not appear in Austen's work, and a way to communicate with them as well. His natural predilections for exploration, investigation, mimicry, and drama, combined with his natural flair for figurative language and his access to nonrational states of mind, meant that he could not help expanding the possibilities of the novel and almost by himself creating the literary world that surrounded him in the early 1860s. But he was, in some sense, now outmoded. Having read his works, his contemporaries saw their flaws —his native deficiencies in tightness of construction and complexity of characterization—and learned from them. Their works were more subtle and nuanced, more private and less convivial, you might say, more focused on the inner life as lived rather than as projected outward. Even so, they existed inside the gates of the very broad world that Dickens had shown over and over was the appropriate home of the novel.

Dickens's public readings, in addition to being a scheme for making money and for performing and for getting a feeling of connection to his audience and fans, were also the next step in the idea of the novel, a step into a territory where other novelists were not able to follow (except in a pale sense that novelists today go on book tours and read more or less skillfully from their own work). If the novel by nature seeks to communicate more and more about a world that contains more and more material worthy of communication, then Dickens, with his rehearsals and his rewritings and his careful projection of his words, was attempting to make every single word count. The ideal would be that every word would be both clear and evocative of many overlapping meanings— that is, the natural complexity of the novel, both overall and sentence by sentence, would be taken to its limit. For Dickens, "meaning" included both large quantities of ideas and large quantities of emotion, so the proper audience reaction would be both emotional and intellectual (a reaction he found in France and in Scotland most frequently). In addition, the mutually subjective writer/reader experience, wherein the reader feels his or her mind is in direct communication with a single other mind, the author's, would also be fulfilled by the staged intimacy of the setting. Nor could the novels be acted out—the author/narrator was essential to the public reading as a novel-like enterprise rather than a more impersonal drama-like enterprise. So even when his contemporary novelists were in some sense disdaining Dickens for déclassé self-promotion, he was testing the boundaries of the novelistic enterprise—that is, the boundaries of how a narrative can be communicated. It is thus no coincidence that his work has some affinity with film, a narrative form that portrays some aspects of modern life more effectively than the novel does.

Between January 1862 and April 1866, Dickens did no reading tours; he did not begin his next novel, *Our Mutual Friend,* until November 1863 (though he thought of several ideas and names that later appeared in it). There is no record of where Ellen Ternan lived at this time, only that she and her mother did not attend Maria Ternan's wedding in the summer of 1863 (though there is no evidence of a breach between them). Dickens worked on *All the Year Round* and traveled back and forth to France, sometimes for only a few days at a time. He even went during the summer of 1862, when Georgina Hogarth was seriously ill. Most commentators believe that Ellen and her mother were in France, supported by Dickens, though no scholarly investigations have uncovered where they were living. Some believe that Ellen had a baby in these years; Dickens's daughter Kate told a friend of hers many years later that there had been a son who died (a story corroborated by Dickens's most successful son, Henry). At any rate, Dickens was depressed, he reported to Forster, and the evidence of Pip and the later character of Jasper, in *The Mystery of Edwin Drood,* show that Dickens was exploring the idea of guilt in his novels. There is no reason to believe that Dickens's feelings toward Ellen, about his situation, and about himself didn't fluctuate over the years. It is not uncommon for a man or a woman to act in accordance with his or her desires, only to find that the accomplished goal doesn't have the imagined results but must be accommodated anyway. Dickens didn't have much experience with being satisfied or at peace. Even if he was able to arrange things as he liked, that may not have worked to settle him.

In the absence of all evidence as to the terms of Dickens's relationship with the Ternans, there is only speculation about the probable effect upon Ellen's life and reputation were she to become Dickens's acknowledged mistress and bear his child, even in France. Those who think she did become his mistress and those who don't all agree that her prospects would be clouded—her career would court scandal (and she had not shown much talent for the stage anyway), and her ability to make a respectable and prosperous marriage would be compromised. Her most marriageable years were passing—she turned twenty in 1860, thirty in 1870. Rationally, she was wasting her prospects, and according to their biographers, both she and Dickens would understand this. Was Dickens thoughtful and foresighted enough to restrain his ardor and remain a loving but avuncular figure in her life, as

Ackroyd maintains? Or was he willing to risk her well-being for love, his or theirs, as Tomalin maintains? And what was her mother, famously respectable and very much in the picture, willing to risk, and for what?

At the end of 1863, Dickens began to write *Our Mutual Friend*. The gestation of the novel was prolonged and difficult, and Dickens was especially concerned that he would get behind the publication schedule—his sense of his powers had diminished since he sat down three years before to begin *Great Expectations* because his magazine needed a serial. He hadn't filled one of his large canvases since *Little Dorrit*, begun in 1855, and for the first time in his life, he was daunted by the prospect. During the writing of *David Copperfield*, he had told Forster rather gaily of entering a stationery store to buy paper, and overhearing a woman ask for the next number of the novel, knowing that he hadn't even written it yet—that was the only time, apparently, he was ever intimidated by his chosen publishing format. While he was working up *Our Mutual Friend*, he complained several times to Forster that he didn't quite know what he was getting at. The ideas he had pivoted upon character (for example, the idea of a man and a woman both scheming to marry for money, only to discover after the wedding that neither had any) rather than theme (by contrast, his first thoughts about *Little Dorrit* concerned the social problems implicit in the phrase "Nobody's Fault," the first title of the novel). One aspect of English life that still annoyed him was narrow-minded John Bullishness—portrayed in *Our Mutual Friend* in the person of Podsnap. Tradition has it that Podsnap was based on none other than John Forster, as

Harold Skimpole had been based on Leigh Hunt, and once again Dickens managed to betray a friend and portray a characteristic at the same time, though tradition also has it that he got away with it and that Forster never revealed whether or not he realized what Dickens had done.

Once he started, the writing was slower than usual—he was working hard but felt he was no longer as quick and inventive as he had been. One number came up two and a half pages short—a flaw that had to be corrected and seems to have indicated to Dickens that he was losing his professional edge. All in all, the composition of *Our Mutual Friend* did not give him the pleasure that others had (though much of the information about Dickens's views on *Our Mutual Friend* is not available, because the final volumes of his letters have not yet been published).

Yet the novel is a delight. The opening two chapters set the theme—in the first chapter, Gaffer and Lizzie Hexam are out upon the Thames, engaged in Gaffer's line of work, which is salvaging from the river. They find a corpse. In chapter 2, gossip about a strange will comes up at the high society dinner table of Mr. and Mrs. Veneering; at the end of the meal, a young lawyer, Mortimer Lightwood, is handed a message. The beneficiary of the will has been found drowned. Gossip neatly defines the circle of the novel—the highest are linked with the lowest, not by an institution (the court of Chancery) or a system (capitalism), but by the much more casual and yet permanent human inclinations to tell a good story and to investigate a secret. As the characters come into relationships with one another, they do so voluntarily, because they conceive an interest in one another. Their relationships proliferate; desired connections lead to undesired connections as well as other desired ones, until everyone is connected, much of London is explored, and the plot works itself out clearly, logically, and with pleasure for the reader. Throughout, the novel is driven by character and style rather than by theme.

If we compare *Our Mutual Friend* with *Bleak House* and *Little Dorrit,* for example, we see that the imputation, in the earlier books, that characters' views and actions are determined by their circumstances is no longer present. All the characters in *Our Mutual Friend* act in accordance with their sense of who they are morally, or who they would like to be; even Rogue Riderhood has a motto—he "makes his living by the sweat of his brow." The good characters, of whom Mr. Boffin is an example, are able to retain a sense of right and wrong in spite of circumstances. Much of the novel turns upon the moral education of Bella Wilfer, in whom those who love her see an inherent sense of compassion and integrity, but who acts in a mercenary and spoiled fashion. Mr. Boffin intends his ruse of miserliness to uncover the real Bella, not to change her from one sort of girl to another. Dickens is careful, in the beginning, to show Bella's true affection for her father—the question is how she will reveal her naturally good nature, not whether she will. Eugene Wrayburn undergoes a similar testing—when he finds Lizzie in her hiding place and has a last interview with her, his motives are still dishonorable—although he is strongly drawn to her, he cannot bring himself to cross the social gulf between them and ask her to marry him. Even after she rescues him and cares for him, he is hesitant and wonders if his moral weakness is, or should be, fatal. But the experience of marriage (as with Bella) and friendship and connection bolsters his resolve, and the novel closes with Eugene at last attaining a moral vision. Instead of the last note of *Little Dorrit,* which has Clennam and Amy subsumed into the "usual uproar," at the end of *Our Mutual Friend,* the principal characters have made themselves a small society of friendship (and prosperity) that is a refuge from the shallowness represented by Lady Tippins, the snobbishness represented by Lord Snigsworth, the blind pomposity represented by Podsnap, and the passion, greed, and criminality represented by Headstone, Wegg, and Riderhood. In short, Dickens has returned to a comic vision of the world, in which choice and agency determine fate, connection is possible, and individuals are able (and indeed required) to understand their true situations and act on them.

Also in contrast with every novel after *David Copperfield,* Dickens explores the postmarital relationships of his characters, developing images of domestic connection. The weddings are not the end. Bella continues to be tested after hers. Her husband tempts her greed, her trust, her dedication to household management, her relations with her mother and sister. These chapters not only allow Bella to win wealth and integrity together, they allow Dickens to expatiate upon his ideas of a good marriage, which he has hardly ever done before. The foundation of this ideal marital relationship is romantic love combined with gratitude; its goal is some sort of substantial "improving object"; it is lived out among a community of like-minded friends rather than familial kin. Eugene and Lizzie's marriage reflects the same ideals, except that enlightenment and strength flow not from the man to the woman, as with John and Bella, but from the woman to the man. What is important here is that in contrast with, say, Pip and Sydney Carton, the reformed characters of *Our Mutual Friend* are allowed to reap the rewards of salvation; their feelings of guilt and shame do not prohibit them from intimate connection. In addition, that salvation takes place in the world rather than in the afterlife.

Dickens has stepped back from his wholesale critique of English society and, in so doing, allows his characters to assert their freedom within what he continues to portray as a corrupt structure. Corruption, he is saying, is a fact of life, but not the determiner of the individual's moral direction. The average man or woman (not just the exceptional Amy Dorrit type) can understand right and wrong. Twemlow, Lightwood, Jenny Wren, Riah, Mrs. Lammle, and Georgiana Podsnap are all required to assume a moral stance against one sort of pressure or another, and all do, and thus a right-minded community is formed within the larger community of fools and knaves.

In *Our Mutual Friend,* Dickens doesn't seem to be pressing grand themes and motifs, as he had in *Bleak House* and *Little Dorrit,* or even *Great Expectations,* and as a result, critics have not always taken this last completed novel as seriously as earlier ones. But in fact, Dickens's style and character portrayal in *Our Mutual Friend* show that his political and social opinions have been successfully and gracefully dissolved into his use of language. At 820 pages, *Our Mutual Friend* is certainly one of the greatest examples of sustained perfection of style in the English language. Examples of felicitous phrasings abound on every page, from the satiric ("A certain institution in Mr. Podsnap's mind which he called 'the young person' may be considered to have been embodied in Miss Podsnap, his daughter") to the comic ("'Who is it?' said Mrs. Wilfer, in her Act-of-Parliament manner. 'Enter!'") to the violent ("In an instant, with a dreadful crash, the reflected night turned crooked, flames shot jaggedly across the air, and the moon and stars came bursting from the sky") to the lyrical ("Up came the sun, streaming all over London, and in its glorious impartiality even condescending to make prismatic sparkles in the whiskers of Mr. Alfred Lammle as he sat at breakfast"). But grace of style meshes with delicacy and complexity of character drawing. Dickens's typical florid repetitiveness, which sometimes works in earlier novels (Mrs. Gamp, Flora Finching, Miss Tox, Josiah Bounderby, Carker the manager) and sometimes does not (Esther Summerson, Miss Wade, the Frenchman Rigaud), has given way to something much more subtle in *Our Mutual Friend*. In allowing for the possibility of transformation in almost all the characters of the novel, Dickens has changed his mind about human nature—he revisits old character types and sees them anew: the Reverend Frank Milvey, clergyman, is a forgiven Chadband. Eugene is a forgiven James Harthouse. Lightwood the lawyer is a forgiven Tulkinghorn. Boffin the miser is a forgiven Scrooge. Fledgeby is Ralph Nickleby brought low, given a drubbing, and peppered into the bargain. Lammle has certain Murdstone characteristics, but when he canes Fledgeby, the reader has to acknowledge that he has his uses. Bella is not unlike Dora. Lizzie is Agnes with strength and initiative. While I don't want to make too much of these similarities, I do want to stress that Dickens's comic vision in *Our Mutual*

Friend is partially retrospective—the greatness of the novel comes from a new vision of the world that more successfully integrates the conscious mind with the subconscious and the individual with the group, and at the same time more successfully integrates all the various parts of a novel—plot, character, style, setting, and theme.

As I have pointed out before, the form of the novel carries several inherent philosophical ideas—that the individual is worthy of investigation; that his or her relationship to the group is always more or less vexed, but that he or she exists only as part of a group; that reality is always subjectively experienced; that the world is so abundant and disorderly that it can be described only in prose; and that stories can be narrated sequentially and understood. A great novel may work against these inherent philosophical ideas, but a perfect novel must work with them—a perfect novel realizes the implications of the form and communicates the author's idiosyncratic vision simultaneously, in an outpouring of language that seems brand-new and just right at the same time. For me, *Our Mutual Friend* is Dickens's perfect novel, seamless and true and delightful in every line.

Even so, *Our Mutual Friend* was not a tremendous success. The first number sold very well—a new Dickens after two and a half years—but sales dwindled thereafter, and the last number sold only nineteen thousand copies. Dickens made about £7,000 overall (roughly equivalent to some $250,000), but Chapman and Hall lost money. Reviewers seemed to love it or hate it—one of the haters was Henry James, aged twenty-two, who panned it in *The Nation*. Modern critics have been divided also, no doubt owing to its differences from those novels—*Bleak House, Little Dorrit,* and *Great Expectations*—that they have most fervently admired. But the modern era has not, in general, been receptive to the comic novel, or the comic view of life, and has also tended to devalue Shakespeare's comedies relative to his tragedies. It takes exceptional grace of style and a steady comic vision to make a comic novel work without allowing it to slip into sentimentality, while at the same time preventing its satirical tone from darkening into cynicism. Some critics have recognized the accomplishment of *Our Mutual Friend,* but others have looked for something that was no longer there—Dickens's former global critique of English society.

On June 9, 1865, when Dickens was returning from France with Ellen and Frances Ternan, the train in which they were riding went off the tracks as it was crossing a bridge near Staplehurst, Kent. Men working on the tracks had failed to post a warning guard far enough away for the train to have time to halt, and seven first-class carriages went over the bridge into the river below. Dickens's carriage dangled over the bridge, held by its coupling to the baggage car behind it. Dickens and the Ternans were thrown into the downward corner of the carriage, but Dickens managed to climb out the window and then procure a key and get the two women out. At this point, he saw the chaos below. He took his brandy flask and his top hat and went down among the dead and injured; he filled his top hat with water from the river and went around, succoring where he could. Some people died as he was helping them; others he helped, only to return and discover that they had died. Dickens was not especially well at this time, but he wrote to a friend, "I have a—I don't know what to call it—constitutional (I suppose) presence of mind, and was not in the least flustered at the time." He persuaded one young man to get himself out from under the wreckage; he helped another confront the death of his bride. As usual, he did not stint himself or shrink from the horror. When it was time to be taken away by an evacuation train, he climbed into the dangling carriage and found his manuscript.

Although he acted in every way calmly and even heroically during the crash, he began within a day or two to suffer from what we would call post-traumatic stress—he wrote little about it in his letters, but to one friend, he said that thinking about it gave him "the shake," and although he continued to travel by rail and of course hansom cab in order to visit Ellen and to do business and give readings, his children recalled later that any sort of unexpected jolt on the train panicked him, and he hated a cab or a carriage to go too fast. He did not advertise his presence on the train or his heroism. He used influence with the railway company to avoid appearing at the inquest, knowing the identity of his companions would be revealed. He did, however, maintain an interest in at least one of the people he rescued, with whom he corresponded for several years.

It is possible that Ellen was injured in the crash, since Dickens referred to her in his letters as "the patient" for some time afterward, and in later life she was said to have an old injury in her upper left arm. Dickens, as always, went on with business—writing his novel, editing and publishing *All the Year Round*. In September, when the novel was complete, he went to France to do some business, returning over the same

route as the accident, perhaps a conscious attempt to overcome anxieties that were growing rather than diminishing.
His health was not improving, either. In France he had some
sort of "sunstroke," which was probably an actual stroke; his
many long walks were taken in spite of the fact that one of his
feet was painfully swollen.

In the fall, Dickens leased several houses. One, near Hyde
Park, was for himself and his daughter Mamie. Two others, in
the village of Slough, he took under the name of "Tringham,"
one for himself and one for Ellen and Frances Ternan. Letters
written by contemporaries to other contemporaries about the
Dickenses' social lives that fall indicate that they were the
subject of at least some disparaging gossip—Dickens's daughters, after all, were allied not only to him, about whom there
were stories, but also to Wilkie Collins, Katey's brother-in-
law, who lived openly with his mistress. Dickens's apparently
successful secrecy about where Ellen Ternan was and what
precisely their relations were did not inhibit society, his old
enemy, from inferring and disapproving.

In 1866, Dickens embarked upon another reading tour,
this time giving thirty readings for £50 each, and he hired a
new manager, George Dolby, who became a good friend and
ally as well as a trusted business associate. When Dickens had
rehearsed with his usual industry and given a few test readings
to friends, they were once again amazed—he was even better
than he had been, in spite of ill health, post-traumatic stress,
and living a double life. He began his tour in March 1866 and
ended it in June. The reading series earned £5,000, though
Dickens took only his £1,500—he had proved his point
about how profitable such a series could be, and the company

that had put on the series was eager to do it again. But the success of the series could not make up for the fact that Dickens spent the summer in worse health than before, bothered by pains and anxieties. Kate became ill later on in the year too. In January 1867, he began again, this time a longer tour, taking him also to Ireland. The traveling exhausted him very quickly, but the reading itself and the audience enthusiasm seem to have energized him enough to go on. The great paradox of the readings was that they gave him something that they also took away. Forster claimed that the net cost was more than he could bear, but without any detailed knowledge of what was going on with Ellen Ternan, it is impossible locate the real cause of Dickens's complaints. We may infer that the ups and downs of his relationship with her affected him from the fact that he had been so sensitive to the unhappiness of his marriage and to Catherine's illnesses and depressions. There is no evidence that he was ever able to reserve his emotions or assume a cool attitude toward his loved ones. If, as Claire Tomalin asserts, Ellen Ternan bore a child or even two who died, and if, as Ellen later told her clergyman, Canon Benham, she came to regret and dislike her intimacy with Dickens during his lifetime, then there must have been some emotional turmoil between them; but no letters to her or from her survive. The readings Dickens gave were more than a success, they were a success without the ambiguities of personal intercourse. The admiration of his audiences, the money he made, and his own sense of accomplishment in doing a consistently professional job in spite of obstacles carried him through exhaustion and the gathering symptoms of mortality.

The temptation was to go on to America, and Dickens began to explore it as soon as his 1867 tour ended in May. He decided to send George Dolby to America to canvas the possibilities, and Dolby left in August, accompanied to the boat by Dickens, who was using a cane. Another temptation of the American trip was that Ellen might go with him (though it's hard to believe that he actually considered this realistic after his former experience of the United States, where he had been forced to give up almost every vestige of privacy). No doubt the strength of his desire dictated the fantasy. When Dolby returned at the end of September, he assured Dickens that there was plenty of money to be made, and although Dickens consulted several friends (Forster was strongly opposed to the trip), he had already decided to go. The households he had to support and the fact that his sons were not making their way in the world meant that earning a fortune seemed a better alternative than not earning a fortune.

Dickens began to plan his trip and persistently held on to the idea that Ellen might accompany him, all through the fall and even until he arrived in the United States in mid-November. Their plan together is somewhat confusing, as if a fair amount of subterfuge was involved. Ellen left England for a visit to her sister in Florence at the end of October. Dickens's plan was to get to America and reconnoiter (he had two weeks before the first reading). If Ellen's companionship looked possible, she was to travel back to England and take the boat from Liverpool on December 11. A coded message, passed to her from W. H. Wills, was to tell her what to do. But it did not look possible—once again, Dickens was beset with appearances and engagements. Ellen, who was staying with her sister, the wife of Anthony Trollope's older brother, made no apparent effort to leave. Possibly she did not agree with his plan to begin with. At any rate, Ellen Ternan stayed in Italy, and Dickens made his American tour alone; his notes to W. H. Wills from America (many of them cover notes for letters to Ellen that have since been lost or destroyed) reveal his yearning for her. Her responses are not on record.

Dickens's second American journey was not the disaster the first had been—Dickens was neither so offended by the Americans nor so offensive in return. For one thing, his public readings were a great success, starting with the first one, in Boston. He read every day or so, traveling from one city to another, mostly between Boston and Baltimore, as far west as Syracuse, but not any farther (the loop to Chicago, Canada, and the West was canceled). But the weather was northern winter weather, with snow and sleet and frigid cold; Dickens suffered from colds, flu, and general respiratory malaise the whole time. From time to time, he lost his voice. His left leg and foot gave him trouble, so that he had to use a cane and sometimes prop his foot up during appearances. The sheer immensity of his appeal was wearing—thousands of tickets were sold, he was continually stared at and greeted in the street, prominent Americans, including President Andrew Johnson, wanted to meet and talk with him.

He had many experiences that entertained and amused him, especially encounters with children and friendly strangers. He made friends and renewed old friendships. His postscript to his earlier volume, *American Notes,* shows a sense of forgiveness. He comments that the United States is a decidedly more settled and refined place than it had been in the 1840s, and that he, perhaps, had also learned something. He writes, "I have been received with unsurpassable politeness, delicacy, sweet temper, hospitality, consideration, and with unsurpassable respect for the privacy daily enforced upon me by the nature of my avocation here, and the state of my health."

The state of his health seemed to revive temporarily with his return to England at the end of April. He went first to Peckham, to see Ellen and Frances Ternan, who had returned from Florence only a day or so before. He stayed there for a few days, then went to Gad's Hill, where, he said, his doctor greeted him with, "Good Lord! Seven years younger!" But there was no real rest—W. H. Wills suffered a concussion from a fall from his horse, and Dickens had to assume his partner's share of the work on *All the Year Round*. Family troubles continued. Katey's husband, Wilkie Collins's brother, was ill with stomach cancer; Dickens's unsympathetic attitude estranged him from his longtime friend. Dickens's son Charley went through bankruptcy proceedings, ended up owing £1,000, and went to work at the magazine (he was married to the daughter of Dickens's enemy Richard Evans, and they had five children). Ellen and her mother moved away from the house in Peckham, possibly evidence that Frances Ternan no longer countenanced the relationship or that the relationship had changed to something less compromising and intimate (this according to Ackroyd). Unable to start another novel, Dickens decided to do another tour, his final tour. This time, he thought, he would do a hundred readings for £8,000, and this time, he also thought, he would do something that all his friends and relations subsequently agreed contributed directly to his death, which was to introduce into his performance the murder scene from *Oliver Twist*.

He practiced during the summer of 1868. One day, according to Ackroyd, his son Charley was working in the house when he heard the sounds of two people fighting. He ran out and discovered his father "striding up and down, gesticulating wildly, and, in the character of Mr. Sikes, murdering Nancy, with every circumstance of the most aggravated brutality." The result, on stage, was by every account electrifying and even terrifying (which, according to extant scripts, was Dickens's goal). One male friend testified to a tremendous desire to scream out, and another, a doctor, warned Dickens that one screaming woman would lead to mass female hysteria. It was a sensation unprecedented on the stage, according to one celebrated actress Dickens consulted, in at least fifty years. But how well we recognize it, and the impulse to do it—surely Dickens's acting out of Sikes's murder of Nancy is the direct ancestor of every horrible mass murder, dismemberment, explosion, and gratuitously violent act that we see in the movies and on stage. Audiences couldn't resist it; the author/reader/actor/impresario couldn't resist it. Once again, Dickens was the first, or nearly the first, to try something that, over 130 years later, is almost routine and yet still discussed in much the same terms that people discussed it at the time—is it necessary, is it healthy, is it too much, is it enough, is it true, and if it is true, isn't it still unsafe for public consumption?

He tried it out among friends in November. Most were horrified. He tried it out onstage in January 1869. It was a great success and became his favorite part of the performance.

He did it several times a week, in spite of the reservations of everyone around him, just as he had always done outrageous things in spite of the reservations of everyone around him. He would assert his freedom to the end. In Edinburgh, as the tour progressed, George Dolby expressed reservations. Dickens responded angrily, "Have you finished?" Dolby then replied, "I have said what I feel on that matter." Dickens leapt from his chair and "smashed" his plate with his knife and fork. At the end of their disagreement, Dickens burst into tears. But he did not stop reading Sikes and Nancy. As the reading series went on, things went more and more badly— he was giddy, he fell and cut himself, he was dazed and tired, his left leg and foot plagued him, he was confused from time to time. His doctor and another both advised him to stop the readings, and, finally, some weeks before scheduled to do so, he did, returning to Gad's Hill Place and attempting to rest.

If Ackroyd is correct in suggesting that there had been a shift in Dickens's relationship with Ellen Ternan, this shift would now be about a year old. In the summer of 1869, Dickens began to think about a new novel; it was far darker in theme than *Our Mutual Friend* and concerned not only a man, John Jasper, who was living a double life (respectable cathedral organist and secret opium addict), but also an affianced couple, Edwin Drood and Rosa Bud, who agreed to end their engagement. It is possible to infer some shadowy outlines of Dickens's thirteen years with Ellen Ternan from hints that both of them dropped, as well as from some of the themes Dickens explored in his last four works. In *A Tale of Two Cities,* Lucie Manette seems physically like Ellen Ternan, but she is still one of Dickens's idealized young woman figures, who functions in the novel mostly to support, comfort, and inspire the men around her—her father, her husband, and Sydney Carton. She has no distinct personality of her own, even less, in fact, than Esther Summerson or Amy Dorrit. This is the sort of young woman all of Dickens's letters during his divorce show that he was eager for Ellen to be seen as, and his ideal relationship toward her, as shown by his role in *The Frozen Deep* as well as the portrayal of Sydney Carton, was a noble, self-sacrificing one. It seems as though, at least at first, Frances Ternan and Ellen's sisters went along with this idea—Dickens as mentor, helper, and protector of the whole family, whose interest in Ellen was marked but avuncular.

When Pip and Miss Havisham, in *Great Expectations,* discuss love in terms of "unquestioning self-humiliation" and irresistible attraction, where the loved one is projected into every scene and facet of the lover's perception and existence (very new terms for Dickens in his depiction of love, which he had always previously shown as a form of devoted, active companionship), we don't have to make Estella precisely into Ellen Ternan in order to infer that Dickens's ardor was seeking a new form of expression with Ellen, which resulted in her removal to France and possibly the birth of a child. That this was followed by a period of domestic contentment, reflected in the congeniality and generous spirit of *Our Mutual Friend,* does not require much of a leap, and toward the end of the composition of this novel, the group decided to return to England. But in the meantime, Ellen's sister Fanny had married into the Trollope family. There is evidence of bad relations between Dickens and Fanny Ternan Trollope in several letters written in 1867, before Dickens embarked for America, and also of self-consciousness on Ellen's part about her status. Bad relations might easily have grown out of Fanny's desire for untainted respectability in her new situation. While Dickens was in America, Ellen lived among the Trollopes in Florence. Though Dickens hoped Ellen would join him, there is no evidence that she ever planned to. When he came back in April, she preceded him by only a day or two, which meant that she had been with her sister for six months, plenty of time for her family and Fanny's in-laws to convince her that, at twenty-eight, her own secret life was harming her rather than helping her. She and her mother moved out of the Peckham house not long after her return from Florence. Although she then saw Dickens frequently, his sadness, her later remarks to her clergyman, and the theme of parted lovers in *The Mystery of Edwin Drood* would indicate that they were attempting friendship. Possibly, too, her compassion for his failing health as well as gratitude for his love prevented a total breach between them.

Every novelist understands that a novel is a conceit, that making up stories gives the novelist the opportunity to try out emotions, ideas, images, relationships, causes, and effects. A novelist might drop Leigh Hunt into a narrative, but he is not taking Leigh Hunt's actual life and circumstances and depicting them as they are—they would not in that way fit into the other fictional parts of the novel. The purpose of the game changes from novel to novel and novelist to novelist, but in general it is to make sense of the ongoing chaos. We don't have to make Ellen into Lucie, Estella, Bella, and Rosa in order to see Dickens's contemplation of her changing role in his life. The fact is that in his last novels, Dickens's views of women deepened and grew more complex. This must certainly be owing to some sort of ongoing interaction with not only Ellen, but also her mother, her sisters, and his own growing daughters.

When his American friends James and Annie Fields visited England in the late spring and summer of 1869, Dickens went all out to entertain them both in London, where he took rooms at a hotel, and at Gad's Hill, where he planned picnics and outings for them. Mrs. Fields was a dedicated diarist and astute observer. She noted that while he was charming, convivial, and even playful, there was a constant undercurrent of depression—"he is a sad man," she wrote. When they departed from the train station near Gad's Hill, she wrote, about their last moments together on the platform, "he in his cheery way making us look and think of other things until the signal came. A crowd had collected to see him by the time we started but he did not seem to see it and the blood rushed all over his face as the tears came to ours. . . ." This is the eternal Dickens, jolly and kind, quick to feel, possessing quantities of natural social grace. But also in July, he wrote a review of Forster's life of Walter Savage Landor (the original of Boythorn in *Bleak House*) in which he said, "The life of almost any man possessing great gifts would be a sad book to himself. . . ." Always, with Dickens, sadness and even despair went hand in hand with laughter, ready wit, and an appreciation of absurdity.

Dickens began writing *The Mystery of Edwin Drood* in October. He complained about the composition and in fact had to rewrite and reshuffle the first two numbers at the last minute because each was six pages too short, but the extant text shows few other changes. It may not have been easy, but it does seem to have come out as he wanted it. He was pleased with it, too. The plan was no longer for twenty monthly parts to be published in nineteen numbers—Dickens and his publishers felt that the era of such long serials was past (perhaps this was the lesson of the low sales of the last numbers of *Our Mutual Friend*)—but, rather, for twelve monthly parts and a shorter, more concentrated story. The contract provided for the death of the author, too. The first number of Dickens's last, uncompleted novel was not published until almost six months after he began writing. No longer could Dickens sit down, as he had with *Great Expectations*, and produce prodigally at will.

Dickens had always been drawn, by what he called "the attraction of repulsion," to murders and stories of murder. Now, partly through the work of Wilkie Collins, Dickens's friend, the murder mystery had gotten rather more formalized, and *The Mystery of Edwin Drood* was planned along those lines. The tone of *Drood* is darker than that of *Our Mutual Friend*, and the storytelling is far less expansive, much more plot based than character based. Instead of allowing his characters to embroider freely upon the theme of their personalities, he moves the plot forward rather quickly, pausing to expatiate more on setting and atmosphere than on motivation. Cloisterham has an intentionally gothic feel—Dickens is always referring to the dead in their crypts and in the churchyard. One character carves headstones and also explores the various secret chambers of the cathedral. Even so, *Drood* is not traditionally gothic or horrible. For one thing, images of death are counterpointed by strong images of youth and vitality and wholesomeness. For another, it is not the restful dead who are threatening, but the restless and dissatisfied John Jasper. Dickens, certainly aware of death because of his various illnesses, portrays it as a kind of circumambient stillness and coldness, a natural winteriness, not light, but not horrible, either. True horror is reserved for Jasper's aggression—he says to Rosa, "I don't ask you for your love; give me yourself and your hatred; give me yourself and that pretty rage; give me yourself and that enchanting scorn; it will be enough for me." The danger is not that a ghost will walk, but that an ungovernable man will commit rape.

Rosa flees to her guardian, where she is almost at once surrounded by three men and two women. It seems that if Dickens had not died, he would have at this point focused upon the ensnaring of Jasper.

Critics have praised the restrained, somber style of *Drood* rather as they have elevated *Great Expectations* for similar reasons, of being Dickensy enough, but not too Dickensy. It is clear from Jasper's machinations that he is the killer and that Rosa suspects him almost as much as the reader does. The only mystery concerns the whereabouts of Edwin's body. Rosa's protectors are all strong, resourceful men. It is hard to see how Dickens could believably deliver her to true jeopardy. Some of Dickens's familiar plotlines—the moral education of a young man, for example—could obtain with Neville Landless, but by the end of the first half of the story, Neville is still a minor character. The disillusionment of Mr. Crisparkle and the comeuppance of Honeythunder the philanthropist, as well as the exposure of Mr. Sapsea, the pompous mayor, are also tried-and-true Dickens themes, but at this point in *Drood,* they are not especially well developed. Heavily plotted novels are by nature difficult to engineer without careful planning and the opportunity to rewrite and rethink in order to tie up threads and bolster implausibilities. Although I admire much of the writing of *Drood,* I don't think the form of the murder mystery is congenial to serial composition, and I think even a novelist of Dickens's inventiveness and genius would have been hampered by the shortness of the rest of the projected story and by the fact that as he would be composing the climax and denouement, the earlier developments of the plot would already be written in stone.

Although *The Mystery of Edwin Drood* is one of Dickens's minor works, it sheds important light on his state of mind at the end of his life, especially with regard to lifelong concerns. Primary among these, of course, is love. Jasper is similar to Pip and to Bradley Headstone in the power of his passion, but his is far more unscrupulous. In *Great Expectations* and in *Our Mutual Friend,* the beloved woman remains a distant and inviolable object. Eugene is a little like Jasper—he pursues Lizzie, but his own ennui, his conscience, and his desire bring him to an impasse. He asks himself whether he should marry Lizzie, but he never asks himself whether he should force himself upon her—Dickens doesn't allow that thought to rise to consciousness. Jasper's desire, on the other hand, is aggressive. In the first six parts, there is no countervailing idea of love—Edwin's love for Rosa is compromised and dissatisfied, Mr. Crisparkle is almost virginal in his outlook, and Neville's infatuation with Rosa has elements of aggression in it, too.

It is tempting to link Jasper with some elements of Dickens's own psyche. He is an accomplished artist leading a double life driven by passion. He is no less a part of Dickens than

Quilp or Carker or all the other villains. It is also tempting to see Edwin as another version of one of Dickens's autobiographical young men, ripe for the painful passage from shallow boyhood to rueful manhood. Dickens and Ellen Ternan seem to have changed their relations in the spring of 1868 from an intimacy to a friendship; perhaps this is reflected in the Edwin/Rosa plot. And then there is Crisparkle, a physical culturist of perfect charity and innocence, also not unlike his creator. It is as if, once again, Dickens is asking himself what a man is, and is looking within to embody contradictory impulses as narrative figures. What is clearly true is that Dickens's experience of Ellen Ternan and his passion for her continued to the end of his life to feed his imagination. At his death he was still working out what a man was, what a woman was, and what their proper relations might look like.

Dickens's works are often seen to be all of a piece—he did a certain sort of thing, or he employed a certain sort of technique, from the beginning to the end of his career. He was Dickensy. In fact, though, Dickens's novels, stories, plays, and letters show that his ideas and his worldview were dynamic, not static. There were things he came back to again and again—for example, the figure of the innocent girl or the callow youth, the figure of the boorish philanthropist or the termagant wife, the large ideas of comic integration or tragic isolation—but he came back to them with fresh experiences and fresh ideas. His novels propose different solutions to the dilemma of incompatibility while his analysis of the dilemma gets more and more complex and refined. The solution in *Our Mutual Friend* is patience, forgiveness, and communication. Unfortunately, the solution in *The Mystery of Edwin Drood* is forever lost to us. Dickens did not "work out" a static *Weltanschauung* that he carried with him from childhood. His vigorous engagement with his world gave him a perennially evolving worldview that was dissolved into and transformed by the richness and idiosyncrasy of his writing style.

By winter 1869, Dickens was unmistakably ailing. At Christmas, he couldn't come down from his room until the evening, and his left leg and foot, very swollen, were giving him constant pain. His left hand swelled and his left eye began to trouble him, too. Nevertheless, after New Year's 1870, he became enthusiastic about doing a last series of farewell readings in London. On January 11, he gave the first of the readings. The performances grew increasingly taxing, steadily driving up his blood pressure until by the end his pulse was 124. On March 9, he had an audience with Queen Victoria. They spoke of mundane matters; Dickens, of course, was required to stand throughout, a hardship. On March 15, he gave the last reading. The huge audience cheered his entrance. He read beautifully and effortlessly (or so it appeared), and the audience cheered and applauded until he began to weep. For the man and his audience, Dickens's readings from his work were, from first to last, an unmitigated success.

Dickens was as active as he could be to the end. He visited Ellen, he dined out, he read parts of his new novel to friends, he planned improvements at Gad's Hill, he continued his mystery, he wrote and directed an amateur play, he went to the offices of *All the Year Round*. The infirm Dickens kept up a round of activities that would have exhausted a healthier, younger man. It left him exhausted, too, which almost everyone he encountered noticed, but the habits of industry and restlessness could not be broken.

There are two stories of Dickens's death. The standard one, related by most biographers, has him at Gad's Hill with Katey, Mamie, and Georgina on the evening of Monday, June 6, after a day's writing. He and Katey stayed up late discussing her career plans. On Tuesday morning he got up at the usual early hour and wrote. Later that day, he was well enough to take a walk with Georgina. On Wednesday, he got up early and went straight to his writing. Katey and Mamie had returned to London. He worked all day, then complained to Georgina of feeling ill at dinner. Before she could react, he began to talk unintelligibly, and when she got to him, he asked to be laid upon the ground. He became unconscious. His doctors and daughters, and Ellen, were sent for by telegram. He was placed on the sofa, never regained consciousness, and died the next day, June 9.

The second story, appended to Claire Tomalin's biography of Ellen Ternan, has Dickens leaving Gad's Hill on Wednesday about midday and going to Ellen in Peckham, where she still sometimes met him. There he collapsed, speaking his last words to Ellen, not Georgina. She then found a carriage to take him back to Gad's Hill and went with him. They arrived there that evening; then the two women carried Dickens to the sofa, and Georgina and Ellen agreed on a more seemly story for relatives and friends. There are only a few bits of evidence for this possibility. One is a story in the family of the caretaker of the Peckham house, that he (the caretaker) carried the unconscious Dickens out of the house. The other is that Dickens cashed a check on June 8 for £22 (equivalent currently to some $700) and was found to have £6.6 in his pocket when he died. He had not given the money to Georgina, because she soon had to request money for house-keeping expenses from Dickens's lawyer. Tomalin suggests that he took the money to Peckham for Ellen Ternan's household expenses and gave it to her there.

At any rate, Dickens was dead, and his death was the occasion of astonishment to those around him. Forster said, "The duties of life remain while life remains, but for me the joy of it is gone forever." Charles Dickens was buried in Westminster Abbey on June 14.

AFTERWORD

CHARLES DICKENS was a phenomenon by any standard. His stature as a novelist—as the paradigmatic "great novelist," whose work is both popular and important—has only grown since his death. But in addition, his very public life—as an editor, democratic gadfly, theorist of capitalism and modernity, doer and promoter of the common good, champion of both the overlooked classes and eccentric individuals—makes him unique among novelists as a wholly productive and dedicated citizen. And on top of that, his strange habit of prefiguring twentieth-century life gives him unusual interest for us. The consequences of his celebrity—his public divorce and his secret life and his obligation to live out his inner life under the gaze of the world—are fascinating enough. But even more so is his readiness to do such things as hypnotize his friend Madame de la Rue and "cure" her mental distress, or to bring Sikes and Nancy to the stage, for the shocking entertainment of all. Dickens's works and his life show the same thing—a vast intuitive grasp of the possibilities of urban capitalist life. His works explore and touch upon almost every facet of modern life (public sanitation, education of the masses, proliferating litigation, social tensions brought about by class fluidity, waste management, high-speed transportation, dislocation of traditional neighborhoods, divorce, the alliance of religion and economic exploitation, governmental incompetence and corruption, the commodification of family and social relationships, even addiction and colonialism). In the same way, his life expresses social mobility, fame, and freedom of action and of thought generally supposed to be more characteristic of our time than of his. His prescience about the nature and workings of established capitalism is like the prescience of Alexis de Tocqueville about the nature of the United States. Other philosophers and novelists and political theorists have come and gone, but Dickens is still with us, reminding us always that the individual and the group are both present simultaneously, never to be dissolved into each other, but never to be separated, either.

Some novelists plow the same field novel after novel. Others map the world. No novelist has mapped so much of the world, right at the borderline where the inner world and the outer world meet, as Charles Dickens. He has inexhaustibly delineated states of mind, emotions, symbols, ideas, the rational life, and the irrational life, but also London and Kent and Manchester and America and Italy and France and Scotland and Sussex and Essex and Norfolk. He is the novelist who comes closest of all novelists to delivering on that illusory promise of the novel—to tell everything there is to know about everyone, and to tell it in an incomparably fresh and delightful way.

For Further Reading

THE INTERESTED READER could well read all Dickens, all the time, for several years. *The Oxford Illustrated Dickens* runs to twenty volumes and includes all the novels, Christmas books, and stories, as well as *Master Humphrey's Clock, A Child's History of England, American Notes, Pictures from Italy,* and selected journalism. Many publishers offer most or all of Dickens's novels in a uniform edition. The Clarendon Press has also published the Pilgrim Edition of *The Letters of Charles Dickens.* Volume 11, 1865–1867, was published in February 2000. At $140 and more per volume, these books are not cheap or easily available, an unfortunate publishing choice! Also from Oxford University Press, the 1999 *Oxford Reader's Companion to Dickens,* edited by Paul Schlicke, is invaluable and packed with information, pictures, interpretations, charts, and so on. *Dickens,* the 1990 biography by British novelist and biographer Peter Ackroyd, is compendious and highly readable, especially good on Dickens's social context. Ackroyd takes a somewhat more benign view of Dickens than does Fred Kaplan, whose *Dickens: A Biography* was first published in 1988. Claire Tomalin's *The Invisible Woman: The Story of Charles Dickens and Nelly Ternan* (1990) will probably not be superseded, simply because Tomalin seems to have unearthed all the information there is to find about Ellen Ternan. The grandfather of all Dickens biographies, John Forster's *Life of Charles Dickens* (1872–1874), was reissued by J. M. Dent in the mid-1970s but is now out of print. Criticism and interpretation of Dickens's works is voluminous, and several journals are devoted entirely to Dickens studies, including *Dickens Quarterly* and *The Dickensian*. The Dickens scholarly industry seems to be an infinitely branching tree, bolstered by films of novels as well as shows and even novels about Dickens (for example, Peter Ackroyd's play *The Mysterious Mr. Dickens,* which ran in London in 2000, and Frederick Busch's 1978 novel *The Mutual Friend*). But the newcomer to Dickens can do no better than to begin with a novel—my suggestion is *David Copperfield,* to be followed by *Great Expectations, Dombey and Son, A Tale of Two Cities,* and *Our Mutual Friend,* in that order, light, dark, light, dark, light, a wonderful chiaroscuro of Dickens's most characteristic and accessible work.